# *Lauriat*

## *A Celebration of Family*

*Lydia Calasanz*

ISBN-13: 978-1-5008-6687-7
ISBN-10: 1-5008-6687-3


Printed by CreateSpace, an Amazon.com Company
Printed in the United States of America


Book Cover Design by Tina Calasanz

For Mama and Papa and the whole Ong family for making this celebration of life possible.

# Lauriat – A Celebration of Family

## Lydia Calasanz

## Contents

# Acknowledgements

Many thanks:

To Tris for your infinite patience and tireless moral and technical support from beginning to end.

To Tina for designing the book cover.

To Espee and Grace for your valuable inputs and for constantly checking up on my progress.

To Eddie and Tess for continuing the tradition of celebrating the memories of Mama and Papa.

# Chronicling Life

An entire life recorded on pictures and videos. From a mother's labor pains until the baby comes out of the womb, and every single day afterwards, parents delight in clicking a baby's every smile, pout, cry, first step, first bite, first laugh, first hug, first kiss, in short, a child's entire memorable moments. Have you ever wondered how this will shape a person's self-image and personality as he grows up? Surely the impact will have a bearing on a whole future generation. And life as we know it will never be the same again.

This is one aspect of life I was not privileged to have while growing up. As a family we didn't experience much picture-taking. Unlike this day and age, there were few mementos of our childhood years. Sights and sounds of family gatherings, mouth-watering aromas of home cooked foods, games we played, friendships we developed, crises and triumphs, tears of joy and sorrow as our family grew in number and years..........these are but some of the images that have been hardwired in our memories. We try to keep them alive in our conversations and gatherings, in the stories we tell our own children, amidst an ever wishful thinking that we might someday come up with writings of their grandmother's recipes so that we and our children could relive these in our own homes. Memories remain vivid yet there are no tangible proofs of them in terms of photographs or videos.

In writing this memoir, it is my wish, therefore, to give tribute to a beautiful family life of a time not too long ago, when pictures and videos were not available. With the use of words, I hope to be able to paint a picture of that time when needs and wants were simple, where love was made evident by the simple act of a mother getting up early to go to the market, cook, keep house for her family and without saying anything show her love for the sons and daughters she helped bring into the world. Or of a father who by sheer will and perseverance ekes out a living to provide for his family in spite of an absence of formal education and financial resources. And yet again of children who strove to study well in school, knowing fully that this opportunity is made possible only by the single-minded determination, industry, and resourcefulness of their parents, borne of a fierce desire to do all within the bounds of a good name above all else.

I hope I do justice to my mom, who, despite being high strung, was extremely loving and protective of her brood. She was a typical full time mom and housewife who loved being a mother above all else. She enjoyed cooking and seeing people enjoy eating the many varied dishes she came up with every single day. I didn't see discontent or regret in her as she attended to the many needs of her big family and shifted careers from an independent woman to a full time mother and housewife.

My father, too, was equally focused on providing for his growing family. His guiding principle in life was summed up in a good name "*mianh shianh*"and hard work. And for him, *tsia si hok* "eating is prosperity". He saw to it that we ate well and that we persevered in our studies because to him, education is the key to a good future for us. In time all nine of us finished college and got good jobs and formed families of our own.

Looking back now, I can see that food was, indeed, the one major binding gel of our family. Like many Chinese people, we loved to eat and we were blessed with a mother who loved to cook. Our family could indeed be likened to a lauriat, a celebration of family.

.

# Introduction

"Hurry up! It's almost seven o'clock! We'll be late!", my younger brother Eddie shouted as he came running down the stairs. The other members of the family were in various stages of getting ready for the annual New Year's Eve celebration of the Ong family. We were going to have a dinner lauriat in one of the more popular eateries in Chinatown in Manila in the sixties, the Panciteria China. Being the eve of the New Year, loud explosions all over the metro were starting to be heard. As is the usual tradition in the Philippines, firecrackers are the one big mainstay of the celebrations ushering in a new year. The louder the sound, the better to drive away negative spirits and bring in luck and prosperity!

As we continued preparing to leave, we could hear the noise escalating. The thunderous popping of firecrackers and the bleating of trumpets added to the excitement. Smoke and smog were slowly starting to cover the air. A lot of people were outside their homes, talking with guests, playing with the children, lighting their own firecrackers. Once in a while a neighbor would light a firework display which explodes in a cacophony of sounds and colors ending in a final luminous shot up into the sky. This is definitely going to be one noisy, fun filled night. Bright colored lights shone in almost all the windows in our neighborhood. Most were adorned with Christmas lanterns of different colors and designs. This added to the festive ambience all around.

The Philippines and especially Manila has always been known to have the longest and the most enjoyable Christmas season in the world. And as a child growing up so close to downtown Manila in the sixties, I experienced first-hand the exhilaration with which Filipinos greeted Christmas and especially the New Year. It was fun and enjoyable! It was good to live within such an atmosphere of cheer and tradition.

Our family lives in a small residential neighborhood just two blocks away from downtown Avenida Rizal. Papa and my uncle "A-kuh" run a textile store next door to the famed National Bookstore and two stores away from Avenue theatre, one of several premier movie houses dotting the skyline of busy Rizal Avenue in the sixties. Christmas lights and Christmas carols provided a colorful, festive atmosphere to the holiday spirits that night. For us children, the holidays were always a welcome time of the year especially when it was capped with a dinner lauriat. I could almost taste the delicious array of fine dishes and treats that was coming. This coupled with new clothes and shoes, not to mention the gifts and toys we received, put everyone in high spirits. A few more minutes and we were all dressed and ready for the celebration.

Since the restaurant is but a few blocks away from the house, it was customary for us to just walk the short distance to Panciteria China. It was fun trying to dodge the firecrackers. Sometimes we would get scared but all in all, we were more thrilled than frightened. Hand in hand, we made our way through the crowds of people rushing to make last minute shopping or trying to catch the jeepneys to home. One by one, the department stores were starting to close shop. And when at last Chinatown came into view, our excitement increased in step with the now more deafening sounds of stronger types of firecrackers. There were still people rushing to buy fruits and Chinese goodies for the New Year's eve. All stores in Chinatown were bright with lights and colorful Christmas buntings. Red boxes of hopia and various sweet delicacies were on display alongside cartons of apples, oranges, grapes, pineapples and many other types of fruits. Dragon dancers threaded their way through stores and their ear-splitting drumbeats blended with the over-all noise and jubilation. Seems like tonight, nobody would be sleeping before midnight strikes to usher in the beginning of the New Year.

And at last, we arrive at the restaurant. We see the name "Ong Family" at the function room reserved for our lauriat. The table was big. It could easily accommodate all eleven of us (our parents and all nine of us brothers and sisters). The floor manager greeted my Pa and we all proceeded to sit down. The hot teapot and the saucers of peanuts and melon seeds were placed neatly on the lazy susan sitting atop the bright red tablecloth. We picked on these goodies as Pa motioned for the manager to start the lauriat.

This is the story of our family, the Ongs, situated in downtown Manila from the early fifties and sixties. I like to think of our family as a tale of celebration symbolized by the traditional Chinese lauriat. My father came from China as a young boy of sixteen with nothing more than the clothes on his back. With sheer perseverance and a lot of hard work and determination, he was able to pull himself up from his bootstraps, developed a small business with family and friends, got married, and sired nine children. Truly, a multiplication of the loaves. And as in a lauriat table, the five boys and four girls grew up to become as diverse and at the same time as unique as each dish on the table.

As is typical of the early Chinese immigrants in the Philippines, my father inculcated in his children the same fierce determination and moral values to succeed in a foreign land. His one enduring principle was that of a good name and a good heart. And he resolved that a good education for his children would be an unflinching goal for him who was not as fortunate to have had one himself. On top of all this, he raised us up with good food and good cheer, for to him, *tsia si hok*, "Eating is Prosperity".

# Growing Up in the Sixties

The sixties were one of the most interesting periods to grow up in. I was in my teen years then. Manila was undergoing a lot of visible economic progress, having emerged from WWII almost twenty years ago. Remnants from the destruction brought about by the war and subsequent Japanese occupation were being replaced by changes inspired by the new political realities. A newly independent Philippines with a fresh vision of governance and prescription for progress and economic development signaled a whole new outlook that was both heady and hopeful. Change was everywhere. In this space in time, life was still simple, yet the air was filled with the pregnant optimism of better things to come. Young people could dream and we were aware that infinite possibilities were totally achievable if we strove hard enough. Robert Kennedy's words rang clear in our ears, "Some men see things as they are and ask why? I dream of things that never were and say why not!"

Yes, we were raised with the belief that if we studied well, all our dreams were within reach. Nothing was impossible. There were nine of us children. My mom was a stay at home mom. My father was engaged in a retail store selling men's textile materials. Like many Chinese men of his era, he believed that entrepreneurship was the way to go. Together with a number of like-minded friends and relatives, he set up a textile store located in the heart of downtown Avenida Rizal. This was considered prime location then. There were the prime movie houses "Avenue, Odeon, State, Ideal" to name a few and the National Bookstore which grew to be the largest bookstore in the Philippines. There were a no. of furniture shops as well as appliance stores, pharmacies, bookstores, tailoring shops, and eateries. One could also walk a few blocks and reach Sta. Cruz Church, a popular Catholic church in the Philippines.

I guess we were lucky in that we lived just two blocks away from here where "the action is" all the time. Throngs of people pass through Avenida the whole day. The mode of transport then is the very popular *jeepney* (remnants of the army jeeps used in the war, and redesigned to be a public conveyance which easily seats eight to ten people at the back). Scattered on the sidewalk fronting the store were scores of ambulant vendors who sell everything from nail clippers, to cigarette lighters, to combs, etc. There was also the keysmith whose tool of the trade was contained in just one small wooden box.

Our store has its front door facing Avenida Rizal. On its side along the corner street was a long stretch of glass windows which provides a clear view of the store's interior. The reams of textile materials are placed standing up and its rows and rows of material stretch all the way to the back of the store where another open door is located. An abundance of thin long rods of flourescent lights provides a clean, bright and airy ambiance.

My uncle whom we fondly call *A-kuh*(First Uncle) manages the store. He is tall, broad built, fair skinned and handsome as they all are on my mother's side of the family. Their aquiline noses as a family stand out. Unfortunately, I was not able to inherit that gene as my own nose is small and the bridge not so high. *A-kuh* can be seen seated on the high-backed chair of the cash register most time of the day. Watching over at the back end of the store was another Chinese man who was also clean cut and kind looking. We call him simply Sun Hee. He likes to smoke his pipe once in a while. Then there is our handyman named Tirong. Always neat and clean, he stayed with the store until it closed down in the late 1990's. Tirong was short and thin but he could carry a lot of weight. His work entails bringing down the reams of cloth for the customers. Rolling and unrolling the reams especially during inventory time at year end would surely exhaust a lot of men. But Tirong carries all this as a regular part of his day. Another old hand at the store was Tino, a cousin of my mom. As is a common trait of Filipinos, he is short of stature. Part of his job is to see to the cleanliness of the washroom and of the floor and of the glass windows. He also serves as the main watchdog at the front entrance. Petty thieveries were a common problem in the Philippines even during those times. Tino maintains that his job keeps them all at bay. This small staff of people stayed on for many, many years. They have become like family to us.

The sixties not only afforded us a wholesome environment to grow up in. It also gave us a lot of freedom to build and chase for our dreams. The streets were still safe for us to walk on to and from school, work, and home.

Mabolo is situated almost two blocks away from Avenida Rizal. We grew up in an apartment here. Crossing Avenida, is a short parallel street and two blocks away is Mabolo. One turns right and here, one sees two rows of apartment buildings facing each other. Together with my eight other siblings we stayed here until we got married one by one in the seventies and eighties.

My mother used to tell me that when they were newly married and had only two children, they lived with my aunt Ebeng and her equally young family in Trinidad street, two blocks away. But when they realized more children might be coming from both their families, Papa and Mama decided to move out and transfer to neighboring Mabolo. Nevertheless, our two families remained close through the years.

"Cheaper by the dozen" seems to be the characteristic motto of the times. Mama's yearly childbirth ended only when we reached the magic number nine. Growing up in such a large brood was fun. There was never a dull moment. Of course we fought a lot too, cried a lot, laughed a lot. This was to be expected since we were so near in age, being only one or two years apart from each other. Petty quarrels and arguments were a common scene and in such instances, Pa was quick to point out that "*tsih na bo nung iyn bue tan*" meaning "a coin always needs two sides to make noise". Mama frequently remarked that we all came from one father and one mother, but our temperaments and personalities were so different one from the other that people could think we came from different fathers and mothers.

Thinking back now, I would say it was a feat for all of us to manage to live so smoothly inside a two storey apartment with two bedrooms, and only one washroom. The house was long and not too wide. The front door consisted of a heavy wooden door that folded into four parts. My Pa later on had another slatted wooden door built over the original one so that we could open it up the whole day and still have some security.

It opens into a living room with a white smooth cement floor. Our living room set consisted of one long narra sofa which could seat four people. Two single seater sofas stood on each side of this long one. Across the room were another two similarly designed single-seaters divided by a small center table. The stairs to the second floor was situated at the wall along this side. It has about three steps and ends on a wooden platform after which it makes a left arc towards the second long part of the stairs. This portion of the house serves as the divider opening into the dining room. A heavy tailored curtain adorns this portion. The antique looking china cabinet stands on the wall before the dining area. Our table is big, as is expected for such a big family. It could seat twelve all in all. It is made of sturdy narra like the living room set. And on the table is a thick glass top. Ma used to put a crocheted piece of table linen underneath it on special occasions like Christmas.

The kitchen is set apart from the dining room by a wall with an open window on top of the wall and another door which could be closed at night. The kitchen can be considered a dirty kitchen because beyond it is the open space where our clothes are laundered and hung to dry. The comfort room is right behind the kitchen wall holding the sink and the faucet. The kitchen is spacious with a red cement floor which the maid keeps buffed and shiny every afternoon after Ma has done her noontime cooking. Here is Mama's little kingdom. Here are conceived, prepared, and cooked the much treasured and remembered dishes that Aling Sion, my Ma, cooked every single day of her life. And for these dishes she is well loved and remembered by all her sons and daughters, as well as her many grandchildren.

We started our life in this apartment without any modern conveniences like the refrigerator. The only luxury we had were the electric fans which our household could not do without. Weather in Manila was almost always hot and humid. And growing up, we always had the electric fan on whether it was in the living room, the dining room or the bedroom. In spite of this, Mama was never without her native *abanico* which her hand instinctively moves back and forth to fan herself. During unbearably hot summer afternoons, Ma would instruct the maid to fill a pail with water and she would scoop out this water and throw it on the sidewalk outside to cool the scorching heat of the pavement. This would cool the air a bit but humidity would send us perspiring again.

Rains brought on cooler days and nights. But the floods that came with the seasonal typhoons meant other problems for the house. When the streets get flooded, water would sometimes enter the house. Mama's remedy would be to place a piece of wood to block the opening in the door. Inspite of this I remember enjoying the days when we were forced to stay put due to the floods and the brownouts. During such times, Ma would come up with meals that cheered up the day. The rain always heightened my appetite and eating was a lot more enjoyable than usual. There would inevitably be fried fish and tomatoes with rice. Somehow eating in candlelight added a certain mystique to the dining experience.


Growing up with so many brothers and sisters made growing up a lot of fun. The blend of male and female psyches and aptitudes was in itself enriching. There was a lot of arguments and bantering but there were never any serious fights. And being a girl, I always felt a certain amount of protection from my brothers. I remember a time when coming home from dinner in Chinatown, we were walking when suddenly a drunk man appeared headed towards us swaying and obviously intoxicated. My brothers quickly formed a line and walked in front of us girls to shield us from any ontoward incidents. That moment evoked a feeling of safety and pride which remained forever seared in my memory. History proved that we could always rely on our brothers for unexpected situations where we were harassed or hurt. One early morning when I was about to cross a street in Avenida on my way to go to the office, I suddenly felt a sharp slap on my nape. I looked behind me and saw a young man running. Stunned and frightened, I went home and told my brother Eddie what happened. He asked me for a description of the man who did it. A few days later, Eddie proudly told me "Good news! Remember that guy who hit you? I saw him today. I cornered him and hit him back and warned him not to do that ever again to my sister!" I asked him if he was sure it was the right guy. Eddie said he fits the description I gave him. End of story.

When we entered our teen age years, Papa decided to rent the apartment in front of our house partly as an additional stockroom and also to serve as the sleeping quarters of my brothers. It was a relief for us girls to at last have the bedroom all to ourselves.

# Snapshots of our Neighborhood

"Mrs. Ong ah! Can I borrow your can opener? Mine just won't work." Estrella says to Mom as she crossed over to our house from hers across the street. Of course Mama obliges good naturedly. Estrella and her family owned a shoe store in Avenida. Right next to their store was a similar shoe store which later metamorphosed into the SM mall we are so familiar with today. Estrella has three children who attended the same school we went to. She was always smartly dressed with well-coiffed hair. I could still remember her perfume which smells like that of an imported American doll.

Looking back and writing about it now, I am struck by the fact that a number of our neighbors in the fifties and sixties were actually store owners in Avenida. The businesses were varied, an optical shop, a furniture shop, an appliance store, an eatery, shoe store and textile store. Most were Chinese and all led simple, middle-class lives.

Most had same aged children as us and over the years, we all became good friends.

Our immediate next door neighbors were a Chinese couple with four daughters, Juliet, Linda, Lita, and Sandra. Linda was a very good friend of mine. We used to listen to the radio during weekend nights. Climbing up our ladder to the lower roof where we hang our laundry, we would stay there, radio on hand, watching the night sky and relishing the cool breeze. We liked listening to the poetry reading of Rolando Carbonell. During Christmas, I looked forward to the big jars of peanut butter which her mom would give our family as presents. I loved it because during that time, the only peanut butter I knew was the scoop I bought at the *sari-sari* store next door. So it was almost a luxury to have it in big jars. Their mom never forgot to give presents to our house helps for Christmas as well. They used to host mahjong sessions during Sundays and we always looked forward to the bowl of *kiampong* (fried rice) which their cook Drucky gives us. It is delicious sticky rice cooked with soy sauce, pork belly, and dried shrimps and topped with spring onions and roasted peanuts.

An old Chinese woman whom we called *Lau-Um* meaning old aunt was one of Mama's closest friends. She has bound feet typical of pure Chinese women and she dresses in regular native chong sam attire. *Lau-um's* daughter Ale was a good friend of Linda. We used to watch tagalog movies together and Ale always made sure that she carries a safety pin with her just in case she encounters bad guys inside the movie house. She has a younger brother Johnny, a chubby fair skinned boy. We always get a laugh when we see Johnny kneeling on a pile of mongo beans as punishment from their Mom for misbehavior.

Across our house was another apartment whose tenant was the owner of an optical shop also along Avenida. I remember their dad used to have a tutor come in every day to teach him tagalog. At least two of his three children later studied to become optometrists as well. We nicknamed the eldest son "Bugs Bunny" because of his two large protruding front teeth. Since almost all of us brothers and sisters were nearsighted, we were fortunate to have them for neighbors because we could always just ask for bits and pieces of spare parts for our eyeglasses. They were always generous enough to give them to us for free.

Another neighbor, Aling Rosa, was also a Chinese woman who baked butter cakes and supplied them on consignment to the numerous diners in Avenida. She has three sons and a daughter. His second son is nicknamed "*Peklat*" because of a big round bald spot on the top of his head which was a result of having been accidentally scalded by boiling water when he was very young. Aling Rosa's husband was fond of listening to classical music and it was usual to hear such sophisticated music wafting from their house.

At the corner of this row of apartments was a big three story building which houses a printing press at the first floor. This was the biggest house in the neighborhood. As a child I always thought that the Filipino family who lived there surely must also be the richest in our area. I used to play with the daughter of this printing press. We would go up to the second floor which is almost like a mezzanine where we could look down at the office below. They have a small number of workers in this printing press.

Across this building and right beside our house was the neighborhood's *sari-sari* store (convenience store). It was owned by a big, jolly Chinese man married to an igorot woman. They have two sons. It sits at the corner of the street, enabling it to open its doors on both sides. It was always wide open. People could just sit down here to eat or to just pass the time. Because the store was on the corner of the street, it provided an ideal solid boundary to the neighborhood. Hanging over its two sides was a heavy canvass tarpaulin which could be put down when the sun is too bright and then put up again when the sun has passed, to bring in the cooler breeze of the afternoons and evenings. One could always count on the *sari-sari* store to carry general everyday items from bread, bananas, margarine, peanut butter, cooking oil, vinegar, patis (fish sauce) to inexpensive toys like plastic balloon tubes, paper balls, playing cards, comics, as well as combs, safety pins, and brooms for household use. You name it, they have it and in small single portions, cheap and affordable.

They open early. As early as six o'clock, workers could be seen coming in and getting their breakfast here. There are stools on steel perches where people who were dining in could sit. Breakfast usually consists of a cup of brewed coffee with one or two pieces of *pandesal* (buns) and a small saucer of either margarine or peanut butter. They also carry a bowl of cooked sardines where for a few centavos more, customers could get a small serving of sardines in tomato sauce with their bread. People come in to buy their morning supplies of freshly baked *pandesal.* Coupled with the fresh air of early morning, the smell of freshly brewed coffee wafting from the store and the houses signals the beginning of another day in the street named "Mabolo". Life was simple then and uncomplicated.

We used to play hide and seek, and the folded wooden doors of the *sari-sari* store come in handy for hiding places. "*It*!!!....." goes the shrill voice of the *taya* (the one who will do the seeking out) with his face against the wall and his hand cupped over his eyes. All the other children would scamper and run to their hiding places. "*Bulaga*!!!....." shouts the *taya* and he would remove his hand over his eyes and start the search. He goes and searches for the other players, and the one he discovers first will be the next *taya*. There are ample places to hide…behind and underneath the trucks parked on the sides of the street, the convenient doors of the *sari-sari* store, and at times even inside the store itself. There was an old Cantonese woman who would sometimes pass by the street. She always carries a cloth bag with her, and to us children, she appears scary. Even then, we loved to taunt her as she passes, and we knew just what was always likely to get her goat….*macau*….a slang for Cantonese. Somehow this always angers her, and she would really run after us flinging her bag! Laughter follows as the children run away from her shrieking in fear.

A seamstress lives a few doors away from our house. She was a short, stout unmarried Ilocano woman. We call her "Manang Dalena". She has a number of boarders living with her, mostly college students. Their house is always open because it is a business place as well. Manang Dalen sewed dresses for a living.

Beside Manang Dalena's house lived a Chinese couple who owned an appliance store in Avenida. Prior to them a Kapampangan old lady with a small grandson lived in this house. The grandma could often be heard calling her grandson "*Boy! Mekeni!*" (Boy! Come here!) Apparently Boy liked to stay for long periods of time outside their house and would go home only when his grandma notices that he was nowhere to be found inside their house. "*Mekeni! Boy!*" goes the grandma. No response. So again and much louder, "*BOY! MEKENI!!*" And this continues a few more times until Boy grudgingly appears from nowhere.

Further along the road lived an old woman who taught me my first catechetics. She was a stern looking dignified Filipina who was living alone. We used to like playing "Step/No" outside her house. And this irritated her because it was usually in the afternoons when she was taking a nap. So, one day she called us over and asked if we wanted to learn religion. Afraid to say no, we stepped inside her house. It was beautifully furnished. The floor was shiny and we were delighted to see a parrot whom she kept in a cage in the kitchen. It could actually talk. Eventually I was the only one who stuck it out with her until the end. Thus, I learned my first confession and first communion. I now forget what her name was but on the Sunday that I received my first communion, the two of us celebrated by having breakfast at her house. And I was more than delighted when I saw hot chocolate and pandesal on the table. It was a treat to sip delicious hot chocolate and it made the day memorable.

At the end of our street was a small unit which houses a warehouse for newspapers and magazines. The sixties were the comics era. I remember waiting at our door for the ambulant comics vendor who would pass by on specific days of the week for the serial Filipino comics that I loved to read. I always gladly shelled out a few centavos to buy these comics.

Bitty, a childhood friend who later became my brother Danny's wife, lived in a house just across the *sari-sari* store. Bitty also went to UST high school and although we were not classmates, we sometimes went home together. There was a time Bitty came home with the bottom seams of her skirt torn. The teacher had slashed the seams because it was too short. We were required to keep our uniforms at least two inches below the knees.

A block away from Mabolo is Trinidad where my cousins live. As a young girl, I loved to go over to their house where I would often play with Tessie who was slightly younger than me. They also had a big family with eight brothers and sisters. I liked to go to their house and lie at their *duyan* (hammock). I understand that as babies they were laid at this *duyan* so that their heads would continue to be beautifully round as the cloth of the *duyan* softly cradles and protects the head of the baby. Another thing that I found exciting in their house was the double decker bed and there were times, I would actually sleep over at their house so I could sleep on the top of the decker. I remember their dad's peculiar practice of drinking water directly from the water pitcher. I understand that he only drank boiled water. Tony, a younger brother of Tessie was also my brother Danny's favorite buddy growing up. "*A-I*" (First Aunt) was how they address my mom, while we call their mom "*Sa-I*" (Third Aunt).

Mabolo street holds in store many, many happy childhood memories for me and my siblings. I didn't realize until now that I am writing about it, that our neighborhood actually housed quite a number of people who owned stores that then populated downtown Avenida Rizal. They were all ordinary, middle class families who were hardworking and persevering. They formed the backbone of the business infrastructure that would eventually flourish in the greater Manila area.

# Aling Sion – Colorful Wife and Mom

To our neighbors, she is "Mrs. Ong", and to her many other friends she is simply "Aling Sion". Pleasantly plump and short at almost five feet tall, she has slightly chinky eyes, a characteristic tiny dimple near her lip, and curly short hair which she keeps dyed black. At home, you always see her in casual loose housedress which we call duster in the Philippines. For my annual gifts to her, I always made sure that the dusters I choose are bright and colorful with flowery prints and most importantly with the must have open square pockets because she likes to have her cluster of keys handy with her all the time. Yes, this is my mother whom I am extremely fortunate to have shared a big portion of my lifetime with.

Mama is not ashamed to tell us that she has not had the good fortune of finishing school beyond third grade elementary because their family simply could not afford it. But she is quick to add that she was at the top of her class during those few years and the school principal even talked to her parents to try and convince them to allow her to continue schooling. But what she lacked in formal education she more than made up for in her generally cheerful disposition and sheer tenacity for hard work and commitment to help send her younger siblings to school. She tells of the time when she would attend bible classes in a Protestant church just so she could receive the food dole outs that came after. Or of the time during the Japanese occupation of Manila when she dozed off while caring for an infant sibling which led to somebody stealing the folded bamboo mat standing near an open window of their room. As a consequence, for many weeks afterwards, her mother would spank her every time the former laid eyes on her.

My grandfather was stricken with cancer, and Mama tells of how for hours she would fan him with the native abanico, and he would still cry in pain because of the burning heat of his body which no fanning could alleviate. During this period, she lost a lot of weight. Her father eventually died of the cancer.

Mama spent a big part of her single years working as a cashier in a pharmacy. This gave her the chance to gain a practical understanding of the basic remedies for simple illnesses. Above their store, a newly graduated medical doctor held office and the two of them became good friends because Mama referred a lot of patients to this doctor. It was not uncommon for customers at the pharmacy to ask for referrals and Mama would unfailingly point to the doctor upstairs who happened to be an obstetrician. And when Mama eventually got married and had children one after the other, this doctor became our family doctor as well.

"Mrs. Ong ah, may I borrow a piece of onion? I need it for my dish and I forgot to buy some." "Mrs. Ong, here is a bowl of sweet dumpling which I made." "Mrs. Ong, how are you this morning?" The neighborhood has become almost one big extended family. And Mama was a friend to one and all. Although she rarely went to our neighbor's houses, there was a comfortable familiarity and all of us children were assured of a wholesome and safe environment growing up.

"Her bark is sharper than her bite." an uncle often remarked when talking about Mama. Yes, Mama can be a terror especially when she has had it with all of our childhood antics and squabbles at home. During such times, her motto "spare the rod and spoil the child" comes across loud and clear. To the house helps, she is likewise strict and uncompromising in her rules. Thus, it is an unusual day when the house is quiet without hearing Mama's voice in the background. It is either Mama is not home or she is not feeling well. But for us, all of these are just the bits and pieces of Mama which make her such a colorful character. We all love her dearly. I remember Carmen, a short pleasant maid from Bicol, who always manages to chuckle nervously whenever Mama scolds her. Being in such proximity to Mama has taught her that indeed Mama's bark is more fearsome than her bite.

After lunch, Ma and Pa unfailingly take a short nap. The maid would roll out the navy cot in the living room. Papa would lie down in the sofa, while Mama takes to the cot. I loved to snuggle near Mama during the times when I was home. When she started having gray hair, she would jokingly commission us to pluck out the grays that were starting to be visible in her hair for a fee. Of course this was just to entice us to do this. We never did get paid for the task. Mama swears that it was during such afternoon naps when she started consuming a lot of "white rabbit" candies that she developed her adult onset diabetes. And for the rest of her life, she has had to inject insulin to manage her diabetes.

During lazy afternoons, we would hear the vendors peddling their wares in our street. I always loved it when Ma decides to buy *nilagang mais* (boiled corncobs). They almost always taste so sweet and juicy. If she is feeling extra generous, Mama would delight the vendor by offering to buy her whole basket of merchandise. This usually happens when the mais are super sweet, chubby and short. I am likewise exhilarated whenever this happens because that means I could eat more pieces. Many times we would settle for the chippies which we would dip in ketchup. During Christmas season when the store stays open for an extended hour, Mama would prepare a kettle of coffee with cream and sugar and *pandesal* with fillings of sardines or hotdogs and have these delivered to the store to help tide the workers for the extra hours of work. Coming home from school, we would go directly to the store for the extra treats.

There are days when Ma would feel like cooking typical Filipino merienda fares like *guinataan*. *Guinataan* simply means cooked with coconut milk. This easily takes the form of *guinataang munggo* which is Mama's favorite or *guinataang halo-halo* or *guinataang mais*. For the first kind, she would first toast the mongo beans on the wok until the toasted beans become super aromatic and brown. Then she would put it on the casserole filled with sticky rice and coconut milk. If she was planning to cook this, she would already buy grated coconut from the market in the morning. At the market, the coconut vendor would first split the mature coconut into two with a sharp bolo, and then he would run it over a whirring metal spike which would spew off the coconut shreds. Once home Mama would put some water into the grated coconut, mash it and then wring it out using a cheesecloth. The first supply of milk would be set aside. Called *kakang gata*, it is thicker and creamier and used to top the finished *guinataan*. Subsequent additions of water would render a thinner consistency. This is the coconut milk that goes into the initial cooking of the *guinataan*. The *guinataang halo-halo* is a bit fancier and more colorful. Plantain bananas cut into chunks, together with sweet potatoes also cut into chunks, *bilo bilo* or tapioca, and shreds of *langka* are boiled in the coconut milk. White sugar is added to make a sweet, creamy merienda fare. *Guinataang mais* is perhaps the simplest to make. Either canned corn kernels or fresh corn shreds are used and cooked in the same way with sticky rice, coconut milk and sugar. I always looked forward to these days when Mama comes up with special treats like *guinataan*.

*Saging na saba* (plantain banana) is another favorite ingredient for a number of popular snack items, *maruya*, *banana que*, and *turon*. Mama likes to cook *maruya*. Slicing the saba banana into four parts lengthwise, she would dip these in a batter made of flour, water, and sugar. Then she would fry it in oil and the finished product is further coated with white sugar. The *banana que* is done by deep frying whole saba bananas and then pouring sugar into the cooking bananas, so that what emerge are golden brown bananas covered with crisp syrupy coating. The *turon* requires a little bit more work, because the peeled banana is wrapped in *lumpia wrapper* and then deep fried in vegetable oil. For a more elaborate *turon*, slices of *langka* are included in the wrap. For a much simpler fare, the saba banana is boiled in sugared water and served with shaved ice and evaporated milk.

Mama is seldom idle. In the afternoons when she has nothing to do, she would take out Pa's socks or *sandos* (sleeveless t-shirts) which needed darning and she would take her needle and thread and begin to do some sewing. She was a handyman, too, and some afternoons I see her cutting the big empty can of cooking oil. She saws it into two diagonal halves. Then she would get a wooden pole and hammer it into the halved can to make into dustpans. She ends up having two dust pans. Sometimes she would fashion out a low stool for the maid to be used for her laundry chores. No task was beyond Mama. When my brothers were younger, she would get some scrap cloth materials from the store and sew up shorts for them. Papa bought a Singer sewing machine for her and I believe that she managed to save quite a lot on our clothes because of this.

After her chores, Mama regularly takes her daily bath. And then begins her beauty ritual. She would put on Pond's cold cream, after which she dabs on her Lorrigan Coty powder. She regularly plucks her eyebrows after which she draws on it with a brown eyebrow pencil. Before combing her wet hair, she rubs in a little Suave hair crème to come up with a neat clean finish. For special occasions when she had to dress up, she routinely splashes on a little of her favorite cologne Channel #5.

I liked to accompany her to her hairdresser once every three months. The beauty parlor was located a few blocks away from Avenida Rizal and we usually went by jeepney. Having our hair curled takes almost two hours and more if the line is long. After we are shampooed, the hair is cut into the desired length. Then, the hairdresser seats you in front of the mirror while she gathers the curlers, combs, brush, lotions, and solutions she would need. The hair is then partitioned into sections, and the curlers are rolled into the hair one by one. After that, she sprays the hair with perming solution and wraps up your entire head of hair with a plastic. A timer is then set. When the curing is finished, the timer goes off. The hairdresser checks to see if the curls are already done. If it isn't, she sets the timer to the required additional minutes and the waiting continues. If subsequent checks show that the required doneness has been achieved, she again puts in another solution which is to end the curing process, after which the hair is washed, and then set. I remember that we would then be placed under a hooded dryer with our ears shielded from the heat by pads. This usually takes another fifteen minutes or so. And after that, we get to the exciting finale, the unveiling of the newly permed and set hair. The hairdresser then styles it, and we're good to go! It was always a pleasure to feel so pretty that one forgets the time and the ordeal one has to go through to achieve the results.

Mama has always been frugal and simple. She is proud of the fact that for a matter of a few centavos, she would scour the wet market for the best bargains. She didn't have extravagant whims and fancies except for the trips to the hairdresser and occasional shopping for "*sapatilla*" (open sandals with heels). Ma has never learned to wear flats except for the slippers at home. The only hobby she and Pa had was the movie nights once a week. This was not surprising since we lived so close to the movie houses in downtown Avenida. They would catch the last full show which usually started around nine and ended around eleven. We always knew when they were going to the movies. After we have had our dinner, they would go upstairs to their bedroom. I was especially a nuisance to them because I loved to go with them to the movies. Once I was certain they were dressing up, I would immediately ask to come along. Sometimes I was lucky to be allowed, sometimes not. Once in a while, they would go watch a Chinese movie in Chinatown which was also only a few blocks away from Avenida. So I got a dose too of Chinese culture from these movies. There were times when we would take a *calesa* (rickshaw) coming home, especially when it was raining. It was during such movie nights that Linda, Bongga, and I first learned to play mahjong. Since Ma and Pa would be away for at least two hours, we felt safe playing by using our thick woolen army blanket as the board for the mahjong tiles. This way we didn't make much noise. And when the doorbell rings, we were as quick to dismantle the board and feign sleep.

The smell of sampaguita brings to mind memories of Papa's daily ritual of bringing home sampaguita garlands for Mama. Every evening, he comes home with six or more of these garlands and Mama would put two of these around her neck and the rest on the crucifix in their bedroom. This gives a soothing fragrance to the house and Mama extends the sweet smell by putting her garlands inside her pillow as she sleeps.

Growing up, we never saw Pa and Ma quarrel in front of us. The one policy in their married life is to thresh out their differences when everyone has gone to bed and they are alone in their room. "You should never fight in front of the children" Ma counsels her married friends who sometimes go to her for advice. "Matters between you and your husband should stay between the two of you. You can resolve issues by talking about it when you are both calm and alone." Although my Pa sometimes liked to tell her in jest that he is thinking of taking Ma back to her mother because she is so high strung. We would laugh out loud. And with a twinkle in his eyes, Papa would hug her and they would both end up laughing. They remained happily married for almost fifty years.

# And They Raised Us Well

Papa was quite tall for a Chinese. He was almost five foot nine. He had jet black hair and deep brown eyes. His hair was always combed neatly with pomade. A mole above his lip on the right side of his face stands out. He was always clean shaven. Papa moves easily with his slim, lanky frame and walks with a smooth steady gait. He carries with him a calm and kindly exterior. I have always felt him to be a supportive figure in my growing up years. He has a quiet strength about him. It is undeniable that he has always been a pillar of support for our family while Mama was the steady harbor.

I was always proud to be seen with Papa, and on several occasions it thrilled me to hear my classmates say that my father was good looking. He liked wearing a simple white polo shirt and dark pants. He carries himself with confidence although he was never haughty nor proud. We spoke Hokkien and Tagalog at home. Papa could converse in Tagalog although with a distinctly Chinese accent. He could understand and speak a little English as well.

Mama on the other hand is fair, petite and chubby. She stands barely five feet tall. Her hair is regularly dyed black and always permed short. She wears the barest make up. A super tiny dimple beside her lip almost at the side of her chin accents her face. Like Papa, she exudes an easy confidence and could carry a conversation fluently in Hokkien, Tagalog, and English. She presents an easy, approachable disposition and was a friend to almost all our neighbors. In those days, our neighbors, like us, lived for many years within the same house and neighborhood.

In spite of her temper, Mama is really soft hearted and generous. My mom was a colorful character and a most responsible wife and mother. She loved to remind us to "*matutong mamaluktok habang maigsi pa ang kumot*" which literally means "to learn to crouch to keep warm while one's blanket is still short". This always succeeds in making me think twice about complaining. Our family might be short on luxuries but we always had enough of the basic necessities in life. It developed in me an outlook that is focused more on sufficiency rather than lack.

We grew up respecting the belt as a tool for discipline. Ma often said that if she didn't love us, she wouldn't care enough to reprimand us, and that we would fully understand this only when we have children of our own someday. She believes that a daughter can manage to pay back her dues to her mother only when she herself has experienced first hand the pangs of childbirth. My brothers especially tasted the whips of the belt. They also received plenty of admonitions whenever they misbehaved. Papa often remarked to the boys when he was super angry *"Di thak khi khachng phang"* meaning "where did all your education go....to the gutter?!" But the depth of his understanding of human nature shows in one of his favorite quotes *"Tsi lang um tsai ianh tsi lang eh tai"* meaning "one can never fully understand the issues of another person". Mama, likewise, gave us an earful every so often. *"Hindi napupulot ang pera sa daan"* meaning "Money is not something you just pick from the streets", or *"Marami ka pang kakaning bigas"* meaning "You still have a lot of learning to do" or *"Papunta ka pa lang, pabalik na ako"* meaning "You're just starting off, I have already returned". Pa and Ma maintained that although they only finished a few years of elementary schooling, both of them were always either the first or the second in their classes. And it wasn't difficult to see the truth of this because they were both intelligent and upright people. We were not given undue pressure to excel, but all of us did anyway. Undoubtedly their teachings took root.

Many a time I would hear Ma telling me in exasperation *"Para kang kumuha ng bato at ipinukpuk mo sa ulo mo"* meaning "Seems like you just took a rock and knocked your head with it". And as we matured into young adults, she would constantly remind us *"Ang pag aasawa ay hindi parang kaning isusubo na pag napaso ay iluluwa"* meaning "Getting married is not like putting hot rice inside your mouth and spitting it out when you get scorched". Wise words which to us seemed like nagging at that time but which in our own old age carried a lot of sense. I remember her telling me when I was a mother already myself that "Children are much easier and fun to manage. You need to simply give them something to eat and they're happy and contented. But when they become adults, that is when being a parent becomes difficult." I never fail to admire how she has managed to let us all go so graciously as we left home one after the other to get married and form families of our own. Maybe it is easier if one's family is big because then, the nest doesn't feel empty so early in the game. Or more plausibly because the experience of having raised so many children has given her a deeper reservoir of certainty that the children she has given wings to can now fly to much greater heights than she herself has ever dared.

Papa's one regret in life was that he never learned how to drive. He could ride a bicycle. But he said he could have gone to more places and done so much more if he had known how to drive. Nevertheless, Papa went about his business without being unduly harried. Mama often remarked that Pa lived his life grounded in maxims. He did not practice any particular religion but allowed his life to be guided by the basic principles of a good name and a good heart. He and Mama were married in Binondo Church, a Catholic church, and Ma said Papa received catechetical instructions before their marriage. If at all, this ritual managed to enrich the basic goodness and values that were already in him in the first place. Unlike other Chinese-Filipino families, our family was not raised on strict adherence to cultural norms and traditions. The one abiding principle that my parents practiced was their good name above all. Their children were trained to be responsible foremost in their studies. This was a goal to which we all worked towards.

When we were kids, Sundays were always a family day. Papa would take us all to eat breakfast at the Panciteria China. We were familiar to the waiters there by then and they were always delighted to see our big family coming in. Siopao and soft drinks were the usual order of the day for us. After breakfast, Pa would bring us to a nearby establishment where we would watch him play pinball. It is a machine where for a few centavos, a marble would be triggered to run down a maze. Pa would skillfully move the machine so that the marble would end up hitting a jackpot. Whenever he wins, many coins would be spewed out of the machine as his winnings. We were his cheering squad whenever this happens. After this, Pa would buy us each a handful of chocolate wrapped in gold foils like coins. That always made my day.

Every so often, Papa would decide to eat out on the spur of the moment or whenever one of the children celebrates a birthday. We would go have dinner in chinatown's many small restaurants like See Kee or Lido. I remember one of my favorite dishes was fried shrimp with crispy ham at the center. We often had *ampalaya con carne* and *sate guma hohun* (curry beef noodles). Pa and Ma get a high whenever they discover an eatery that is both delicious and cheap. They call these discoveries "*siok ko kiok*" meaning cheap and delightful. Ilang Ilang Restaurant was one such restaurant. One of its specialties then was the pig intestines which they prepared asado style. Paired with their fried rice, it was always a hit with us.

When children's Disney movies were playing in the downtown cinemas, Pa sometimes took us there. A come on for these shows was often the soft drinks that went with it. Before we go inside, the usher would hand each of us a bottle of soft drinks. Pa also enjoyed taking us to see the circus whenever it came to town. It was always a breathtaking experience for us to watch the performers doing their trapeze acts. We also delighted in watching the big elephants and the lions which were almost always part of the show. In my child's eyes, this was a totally magical world.

When I was in my fourth year high school, Papa bought a second hand yellow Chevrolet car. This was the very first time we ever owned a car. Our driver was a man named Santos who also stayed with us for a long time. Santos knew the streets like the palm of his hand and Papa delighted that we could now go around the metro freely and more comfortably. And he admired Santos for being skilled with driving as well as directions. Mama also found Santos handy with fixing her kerosene stove and helping out with little repairs inside the house every so often. When Papa allowed the driver to sleep in after working with us for sometime, the family would regularly drive along Roxas Boulevard in the evenings to take in the sea breeze along the bay and eat pork barbeque in the many small barbeque stands that sprouted along the boulevard. There was one time we had to rush home to be able to be back by midnight before the New Year. Papa and Mama always made it a point for the family to be home by the strike of New Year. And hooray!!! We made it by a few minutes. Part of our family tradition is to open wide all the windows and the cabinets and put on all the lights inside the house when the clock strikes twelve. Then Mama would carefully place some dollar coins which she had saved during the war on their bed. And as we greet the New Year, we would make as much noise as we could in the belief that this would bring in good luck and prosperity.

As we grew older, we were required to pitch in at the family store, and Papa paid us an allowance out of his own pocket. Almost all of us studied at the University of Santo Tomas for our college degrees, and at that time, block schedules were the norm, so that if you had a morning session, your afternoon was free, and vice versa. That left us free to work either in the morning or in the afternoon. So we were all working students while taking up our different courses in college, which gave us a toe in to the working world as well. Fr. Jette, our parish priest and a good family friend, was often amazed at how our parents trained us all to be extremely responsible individuals although he worried that we might turn out to be regimented.

Like many Chinese, however, we were not expressive when it comes to showing our affection. I don't remember us greeting each other with a kiss or of kissing the hands of our elders as a greeting. In that sense, we might be considered undemonstrative. But primary in our code of conduct is the respect we accorded our parents and the instinctive obedience we exercised as children. The connectedness was there in spite of the lack of external expressions. When Danny became a doctor, I often saw him and Mama talking and it was almost always on the cases he was handling as a pediatrician. Because of Mama's exposure in the pharmacy, she was an eager audience to Danny's stories about his medical encounters and that cemented their relationship in a special way.

Papa and Mama took their goal seriously, that of providing for their children and seeing to it that we all finished college. More than this, however, I was awed at how they lived out the adage that *"all work and no play makes Jack a dumb boy"*. Sundays were always a time to unwind and relax. Nor did I ever see them being unduly worried or problematic. I guess they knew how to leave the rest to God after they have done what they knew best how.

Papa, Mama, and my brother Danny

# Our Family

The love story of Mariano and Sion started after the second world war in Manila. Sion's family had a little laundry shop and Mariano would have his clothes regularly laundered there. Oftentimes, Sion's younger sister Ceria tended the shop but Sion would once in a while take her turn at the counter when she wasn't working at her regular job at a pharmacy. She noticed that Mariano was coming too often for comfort when she was on duty. She thought he was courting Ceria. But soon enough, he formally courted Sion. Mama told him she couldn't get married yet because being the eldest in their family, she needed to help send her siblings to school. And when Papa agreed that he would help Ma in this family obligation, Sion agreed to marry Mariano.

Mama liked to tell us that when Pa and she first got married, she was earning more than my Pa. As a single working woman, she had the luxury of buying a new pair of shoes every so often and was always well groomed. But once she started having children, she and Papa decided that she would resign from work and would devote her time fully to the house and the children. She learned to use "*bakya*" (wooden clogs) when she went to the market and gone were the shopping sprees she used to enjoy as a single woman.

I have a family picture when there were only five of us children. It was a studio shot. It shows my Mom in her classic hairdo of that time with curly bangs and a shoulder length hair. She was quite short (less than five feet tall), and she claims that she never did learn to wear flats because she has grown so used to wearing high heels. My papa was tall, around five feet nine inches, much taller than my mom. The picture shows him in a smart, white suit. They're sitting on a sofa with Mama holding little Eddie, and Papa holding Danny, while I (the one with the teary eye), Linda and Bongga were standing in between Ma and Pa. Linda and I were both in ribbons, very girl-like, while the boys were in formal Sunday garb. I must say we were a smart looking family. We have never been big on picture taking. And this photograph is one of the very few mementos of my childhood years.

Growing up in a large family is quite fun. It's like being part of a community big enough to be noisy and raucous and yet small enough to be interesting and diverse. It also provides a living platform for learning how to survive and co-exist in an environment where one is forced to stay put 24/7. A lot of social skills are acquired and at the same time we learned to give and take a lot. I would think that children in a big, nurturing family turn out very well, indeed, in adulthood.

My mother gave birth every single year. She used to tell us jokingly that if they had known about family planning before, she and Pa would most probably not have had so many children. It takes a lot of energy parenting five boys and four girls. But my mom seemed content with her life. I think a large part of it is because she really loved to cook and it gave her so much satisfaction to see people enjoying the dishes that she cooked.

The eldest in the family is Linda. Now she is a real gutsy girl. I sometimes felt growing up that she was tomboyish. There was a time when my brothers had a fight with the boys across our house. Being boys, they fought it out in the streets. Without a moment's hesitation, Linda rushed out of the house armed with a leather belt to join the spree. That's how spunky she was as a kid. She was also a *Lola's* girl. She loved to go to my grandma's house and when the time comes to go home, she wouldn't budge. Ma had to bribe her with a trip to Central Market where they would snack on *halo-halo* and *palabok*. I also loved to visit my grandma's house because of the long rows of Perry Mason pocketbooks of my uncle Luming. I was an early fan of Perry Mason and when uncle Luming died, grandma gave me some of his collection. Later on when my *Di-E* (second aunt) had children, I enjoyed going to the upstairs room of my grandma's house where *Di-E* and her family lived because I was so enthralled by their tea sets. I never had such lovely toys to play with at home. On top of that, I liked their anchor butter. I always thought Anchor butter tasted better than Dairy Crème which was what we had at home. A favorite merienda that my grandma liked preparing for us whenever we visited was a simple porridge she usually made. She would sauté garlic, onion, dried shrimps, uncooked rice, and *patis*, and then fill up the casserole with water. After thirty minutes we have tasty hot porridge waiting for us at her table. Grandma was a very pretty little lady with extremely fair, smooth skin. She was a lovely woman who aged gracefully. Like many old Filipinas of her time, she liked to chomp on betel nut and lime which makes her mouth bright red. She would also occasionally smoke local brown cigarettes with the lighted end inside her mouth, peculiar habits which I never did understand. Like my grandpa, she also died of cancer.

Linda and I were best friends when we were teen-agers and would often go shopping at nearby Carriedo for our shoes and bags. That's one of her most favorite pastimes, window shopping. She goes shopping whenever she's happy and oftentimes too when she is sad. We had very different tastes when it came to shoes, but I almost always bowed to her sense of style in clothes. She seemed to have an innate ability to visualize what design from a fashion catalogue would fit a particular piece of clothing material, an area I felt I had no aptitude for whatsoever. And before the advent of RTW (ready to wear clothes) one always ran the risk of choosing a style which doesn't turn out good after the seamstress has finished sewing it up. It was, therefore, a relief that eventually, off the rack clothes became the norm.

Bongga is our eldest brother. I guess one could say he fits the popular boy next door image of being tall, dark and handsome. He excelled in high school stage plays where one time he played the lead role of "Cyrano de Bergerac". That particular play left a mark because he had to wear a long artificial nose for his role. And we had to buy tickets to see it. Aside from plays, I remember seeing him in folk dance presentations in school. He could do a *"tinikling"* quite well, which required some skill and adeptness because one had to execute dance steps while hopping over two long rods which two other parts of the team rhythmically tap open and close in step with the music. Once, I was absent from school for a whole week because of stomach flu. When I went back to school, Bongga carried my bag for me and I was elated when my classmates saw him as we entered the room. I could feel myself announcing to one and all "This is my big brother!" I guess that must have been the time when he was a star in campus.

Danny was my favorite brother. He came after I was born. As a child, Danny was extremely clean and neat. He had his shoes on all the time. I never heard him causing any trouble within the neighborhood. Our nanny then, an Ilocana by the name of Juaning, must have passed on the cleanliness habits to the both of us. Ilocanos in the Philippines are known for their frugality and cleanliness. This maid stayed with our family from the time I was born until we became nine in all. Feeding us our supper every night, I remember us kids sitting around in a circle, while Juaning would feed us sushi style. She would make a ball of the rice, fill it with deboned fried fish, dip it in soy sauce, and then drop the rice ball into our mouths, clean, exact, and no mess at all. Imagine this was in the fifties when sushi was not even heard of in Manila.

Danny would later on become the doctor of the family. It was always a heartwarming sight to see Danny with a group of his classmates all in the white garbs of medical students coming to the house during Danny's birthday celebrations. Danny was clearly Papa's favorite. On several occasions I would hear Pa telling Danny that he should always remember that, as a doctor, his primary mission is to heal. Practicing medicine is not like other businesses where the goal is profit. I can hear him reminding Danny over and over that he should not hesitate to treat the poor for free. Danny carried this mindset with him as he moved on to his specialization as a pediatrician. He had a knack for reviving prematurely born babies and thus became a pediatrician of choice by many couples. He knew his stuff well. People felt that he was a true doctor at heart who didn't go by the books. That is why when he finally established a clinic in downtown Chinatown, his practice grew largely through word of mouth. His clinic was open Monday to Saturday and was always packed full of patients. Even the parents and grandparents of his patients oftentimes ended up being his patients as well.

All his nephews and nieces and there were quite a number of them automatically became his patients free of charge. And not only our children, but all of us together with our spouses and also our aunts and uncles and cousins consulted with him. He was generous with his time and service. Sundays would also see him making rounds at the hospitals he was affiliated with. He gained prominence in the pediatric community and was well liked and respected by all. He didn't need to publicize, because his patients spread the news of his competence far and wide. In spite of this, he found time to give free consultations to the poor people of our neighborhood which he still frequented even after he has moved out. Unfortunately, his punishing work schedule caused his early death at the age of fifty-three. He died of a heart attack which ran deep in our genes. His wake which lasted a week was full to over brimming every single night with his patients, rich and poor. That was the only time we learned that he was quietly serving the poor without fun fare all this time.

Eddie was my brother who came after Danny. He was the real boy next door type. Girls used to run after him. He's slim with big, beautiful eyes. He was my constant companion to high school parties because he loved to dance so much. And he was good too. But he got in trouble in the neighborhood a lot. I guess that's why I remember Ma spanking him a lot. Eddie is a happy go lucky guy which he still is until now. Of course he has lots of friends. Whenever my brothers get in a spat with their play buddies in the neighborhood, Mama would at times go to the house of the other boys to inquire what really happened. She always says that if his sons were the culprits, she would surely discipline them. I guess, Eddie must have been naughty when he was a kid because he got spanked a lot. Mama had the habit of saving her energies when it came to our misbehaviors, by oftentimes letting things stride. But once in a while, something would strike a chord in her, and all hell would break loose. Having reached her saturation point, Mama would start calling every single one of us kids. And you better brace up, for long forgotten misbehaviors would be cited and the expected spanking would follow.

During such times, words of fellow buddies would get around and if Eddie was anywhere outside the house, he would be told "Your mom is angry. You're being called! Better go home now!" I can imagine Eddie during those times panicking to go home. And with mom out of sight, Eddie would scamper for a hiding place inside the house. The easiest places to go to are the cabinets upstairs. He would squeeze inside behind the clothes. Praying to high heavens that he wouldn't be found out, he would hurriedly close the doors. But knowing Ma, she knows all our tricks and favorite hiding places. So, opening the door of the cabinet, she usually found Eddie. And the rest is history, a few swats with the leather belt. Ouch! Not only Eddie got spanked, all of us did. After Mama has spent her ire on everyone, things would quiet down. Another day of reckoning has passed.

And then we have the twins, Espee and Carol. They are fraternal twins and were born hours apart. Espee came out first and after an agonizing six hours later, Carol followed. Ma had a difficult time delivering them. Mama used to tell me that oftentimes when she went into labor, her pains had the habit of disappearing when they transferred her to the delivery room. This would go on many times. So from the labor room to the delivery room and back again. What Papa did was to give her "*koh-lè*" (a Chinese herb) which she would bite on to help raise her strength. But with the twins, she lost a lot of blood. It was getting more difficult to give birth. Mama had to leave them in the hospital nursery in order to recuperate. Carol was born a blue baby and so had to be put in an incubator. The twins stayed in the hospital for close to a month. When Mama went back to get them, Espee and Carol refused to go with anybody who was not dressed in white, having gotten so used to just nurses taking care of them. So Ma and Pa had to dress in white in order for the twins to go to them without crying. The nurses at St. Luke's have also grown to love them. This was probably the first St. Luke's hospital in Manila, which was then just a small wooden facility beside St. Stephen's where we all studied. When the twins came home, it was funny to see some of the habits they had acquired in the nursery. They would pick their noses, with one finger inside the nose, and the other three fingers inside the mouth. They would be sucking on their mouths while picking their noses at the same time. We used to laugh at this sight so much. They were already big when they got rid of this habit.

The twins brought much joy to the family. Ma loved to dress them up in identical garbs, complete with ribbons and dainty dresses. It was a delight to see them growing up because they seemed inseparable, and their special bond endured well into adulthood. While both of them did well in their studies, Espee managed to be in one grade class higher than Carol probably due to an accident that required that Carol stay home from school for one whole semester. Their temperaments were also different. Espee is more sober while Carol got my mom's fiery temper. She was also smaller and frailer than Espee. The courses they took complemented this difference in personalities. With her generally happy outlook in life and easy compassion for the poor and the sick, Espee thrived in her nursing profession. Carol, on the other hand, with her outgoing personality and a fearless temperament was much suited for the entrepreneurship course she took and this fitted in perfectly with her life as a partner in her husband's business.

Bobby came next. He was quite good looking too. He has a tall, aquiline nose and small lips. His eyes are nice, chinky looking. Among us all, he was the quiet type. He didn't talk much. But one could immediately sense a deeply principled person, hard on himself and on others. I remember him getting a little pet duckling when we were small. At that time, Ma had a pet dog named Shep. One morning, Bobby woke up to find his little duck dead. The dog had bitten it. He was so mad at the dog we could literally feel his anger. In the end he just cried. Oftentimes, when he was washing his face at the kitchen sink, nobody could get up the courage to ask him to hurry up. He approached me once and asked if I could write his term paper for him. I told him he needed to do it himself, but I would gladly correct his paper after. I was happy when he agreed that this was the more proper thing to do. In spite of his seemingly snobbish exterior, Bobby had a funny side to him. He liked teasing his nephews and nieces and would oftentimes invent funny nicknames for them. A favorite game he invented was *"untog ulo"* (knock heads)which requires his nephews and nieces to bump forehead to forehead with him as a form of greeting and comradeship. Bobby was the last sibling I had to see through kindergarten.

The youngest of our brood was Enyong as we loved to call him. He was chubby and very cute as a baby. When he was born, Mama again lost a lot of blood and her obstetrician advised her that she definitely had to be ligated or risk dying the next time around. And Mama did get hysterectomized before leaving the hospital. Of course, being the youngest, Enyong was easily Mama's favorite. When he was small, a photographer saw him and got Ma to have his picture taken for free. The big framed picture of our cute baby brother stood proudly in our living room for a long time. He grew up to be a mild tempered child. Later on, Mama could always rely on him to fix little things inside the house that needed fixing. He always abided good naturedly. He was the little handyman of Mama.

I have painted a brief picture of our big family, five boys and four girls, each with his unique temperament and aptitudes. But all of us grew up with a strong sense of family. My parents gave us all they could in terms of basic needs and a good education. We knew we were not rich, but we were also aware that the future was good. We ate well, we celebrated life, and we cared for one another. We were happy in our diversity. Like the different dishes in a lauriat, we were a picture of family and a celebration of life.

# Off to the Market with Mama

The round clock on the wall says six o'clock. I am awake, dressed and ready to go. Yes, I am eagerly waiting for Mama because in a short while, we would be going out the door and on to the market. Going to the market very early in the morning always held such a fascination for me as a kid. I love the crispness of the morning breeze. It is that time of day when the sun is just peeping out and the air is still a bit cool and slightly wet with dew. For my mom, going to the market is a daily ritual. With her round native abaca woven basket, and clad in her wooden clogs, she starts her day without a written list of things to buy. But in her head, she already has a menu written up for the day's dishes. All of this depends on what she will actually find in the market and the final outcome determined by the budget contained in her small purse.

"Ma, are we going to wait for all the cars to finish passing before we cross the street?" I jokingly chide my mom as we cross Avenida on our way. Mama is always extra careful when she crosses the street. Avenida even at this early hour is already teeming with utility *jeepneys* and cars. It is a main thoroughfare and is the route leading to Escolta, Quiapo, Taft Avenue, Chinatown, Luneta, Roxas Blvd, and the other centers of commerce in Manila. There are also churches and schools which cradle this part of town.

We walk past our store along Soler Street and pass by numerous small stalls selling imported cigarettes, chocolates, and men's undershirts. Further along, we see *calesas* and more *jeepneys* and buses. The hardware stores and lumberyards that line this stretch are also just starting to wake up. At the very end of the row, we are greeted by the wide open stores selling a big assortment of ceramic tiles, mirrors, and toilet bowls of varying shapes and colors. And we finally arrive at Arranque Market. It occupies literally the whole block on the opposite side of the street. Here, one could buy the freshest and the best meats, seafoods, and vegetables in Manila. This was my mom's daily destination. It was also Chinatown's most popular wet market.

It has been over fifty years when I used to frequent the wet market with Ma, but I could still see it so clearly in my mind's eye. Wet markets are a far cry from our modern supermarkets and groceries. They were always wet, hence, the term wet market. Here, one didn't walk on tiled floors. One had to be careful walking, because the ground was uneven, rough, and cemented with crevices here and there. Every so often, the fish vendors could be seen sprinkling water on their wares to make them appear fresh. Incandescent bulbs light up each stall. For almost the entire morning, crowds of people could be seen making their way here, where buyers and sellers haggle, make bargains, and touch base.

The first part of Arranque is reserved for the fish and seafood vendors. There are three rows of long continuous table shared by the vendors. It is covered by a thin stainless steel sheet on top. Each seller occupies about a meter length of this space. And their wares strike one as a colorful, yummy array of different catch of the sea. We see all kinds of fish varieties. There are *lapu-lapu*, *bangus* or milkfish, *galunggong*, *dalag*, *hito*, and squids, shrimps, scallops, shellfish of different shapes, sizes, and colors…you name it …they have it. The prices vary depending on the size and freshness of the product. I especially like the super tiny shrimps which my mom used to buy and prepare into a fermented shrimp paste we call *"bagoong"*. She is well known in the neighborhood and within family circles for her recipe of *bagoong*. Mama buys four or five pieces of different varieties of fish which are weighed in the scale and wrapped in old newspapers. Plastic bags are unheard of. And nobody has ever questioned if the newspapers were fit to be used as wrappers for food.

Arranque market carries a wide assortment of seafoods, from the high priced live *lapulapu* and prawns to the cheaper varieties like *galunggong*. During the martial law era in the Philippines, the government often prided itself with keeping the price of the GG fish (*galunggong*) within the reach of the poor. Live *lapulapu* was commonly bought by the Chinese for faster recuperation from surgeries, and is also standard fare in more expensive lauriats. Within Arranque, one could get a glimpse of just how rich the Philippines is in its natural bounties of land and seas.

From the seafood stalls, one enters the produce section of the market. My mom buys fresh eggs here. A Chinese man tends this stall. He has a hanging yellow bulb which is always lighted. He scans the eggs that one chooses over this light, to see if it is still fresh or not. One buys eggs by the pieces . These are then placed in papers that have been cut and glued like open envelopes. Oftentimes, this chinaman would delight my mom by giving us eggs which he claims have twin yolks inside for good fortune.

Different varieties of vegetables are available in this section of the market. My mom has her *suki* (favored seller) who always seemed delighted to see her. And she would often sing in a joking manner "Here comes *baratsibong…baratsibong…baratsibong*" (meaning a tightwad). Mama would good naturedly laugh this off with her remark "I might be *barat*, but you love having me because once I buy from you, you're finished selling in no time at all because of the good fortune I bring". And we would all laugh out loud. In tagalog, Mama calls herself *"magaan ang kamay"*. This means a buyer with light hands that draws in more buyers.

At the corner of the dry goods section was the dress shop of my mom's seamstress. RTWs or ready to wear clothes were unknown during those times. The practice was one buys the cloth, finds a design for the dress from the catalogues in the dress shop, and have oneself measured for the outfit. One often had a favorite seamstress to where one goes regularly. My mom's *suki* was Liling. She was a procrastinator. Whenever she gives you a due date for your finished dress, you could be sure you would be disappointed. It was not uncommon for my mom to have to make two or three trips to finally get her finished dress. But she liked Liling because of her skill in cutting the cloth to make it fit the design without asking you to buy more of the cloth.

Along the side aisles, one enters the section which sells abaca slippers and fans, housedresses, brooms, dishwares, pots and pans, etc. And occasionally, Mama would chance upon the vendor of native delicacies. I enjoyed this part a lot because I always looked forward to eating the rice cakes and the sticky sweets which we buy. These are placed neatly in a "*bilao*" or native flat basket lined with banana leaves. When you buy a slice, the vendor would wrap it in a small cut sheet of banana leaf and top it with grated coconut. During such times, I couldn't wait to go home to get a bite of it.

From the dry goods section, we reach the meat section. Here, the atmosphere seems drier. There are also individual vendors with slabs of pork and beef. The pork always came with skin on. We buy the meat by the kilo. Slabs of pork and beef are secured in iron hooks and hung on the steel rods above the stalls. There are also sausages strung together in thin threads. We buy this by the kilo as well. These are minced pork which have been seasoned with salt, pepper, sugar, vinegar, and food coloring. They appear pinkish and delicious in appearance. Dinner with rice and fried "*longganiza*" as these sausages are called was always welcome in our house.

At the end of the meat section is the section that sells innards and fresh blood of pigs. The chunks of blood are laid on clean, white tiled counters. I can't remember where they put the blood that is also measured in kilos when we buy it. The one thing I remember though is that when we buy this and put it in Ma's basket, it usually drips and leaves a trail of blood as we walked back home. Gross!

There were no plastic wraps then, so most of the things we bought were wrapped in old newspapers or used bondpapers. I guess people then didn't know enough of the toxic lead in newspapers. Perhaps the freshness of the meats and fish more than made up for this glaring no-no in packaging. And it is true the meats are so fresh that one good way of cooking pork is just to steam it whole - skin, fat, and meat. The result is delicious complete with the drippings. Mama would let the cooked pork cool down. We usually had this dish for dinner. She would cut the pork into thin slices, making sure to start with the skin, the fat, and then the meat. Delicious! We used to just dip it in soy sauce.

At the end of the market is the *carinderia* or the eatery section. Here, one could have a variety of ready cooked dishes like *arroz caldo*, *palabok*, rice, fried fish, barbecue, etc. Food was cheap and relatively clean. We could also buy *chicharon* (crispy fried pork skins) and a variety of pork intestines prepared in the same way as the *chicharon*. Food! Food! And more food galore.

But we aren't finished yet. As we exit the market, along the fringes are the sections selling different kinds of live poultry. They're kept in bamboo cages. There is an assortment of chickens, ducks, and pigeons. Here, flying chicken feathers are a constant sight. Once in a while, Mama would buy a live hen. She would grope the neck to feel if it is fat. When the haggle ends, she would give me the chicken. This is something I truly didn't like. Ever afraid the chicken might cackle or bite, I would hold its bound legs as tightly and as quietly as I could so as not to disturb it.

As we continue to walk on, we come to the Chinese grocers where an assortment of Chinese preserved vegetables and tofu are on display. We could buy our cans of salted black beans, preserved cucumber, noodles of different varieties, rice wine, etc.

And as we wind up our market day, we again come upon vegetable vendors who have their wares laid right on the sidewalks on sheets of newspapers. Alongside them are fruit vendors with bananas, mangoes, pineapples, *santol*, *guyabano*, and other fruits in season. Mama picks up a bunch of *lakatan* bananas. Usually, this is also the instance when Ma remembers one more thing she absolutely needs to buy. As a favor to me, she would leave me at the Chinese grocer to save me the additional trip. I call the owner of the grocery *"Payat"* meaning thin. I would wait there and continue my assimilation of this noisy, happy, and totally unique panorama of Manila's daily wet market scene. Truly a wonderful way to wake up to a new day!

# Home from the Market

After almost two hours, Ma and the maid and I are finished with our marketing. We are ready to walk back home. The sun is already up. The weather has turned humid. And there are more people up and about in the streets now. The stores which were closed when we passed by two hours earlier are now starting to spring to life. The wooden doors and the steel gates of the hardwares along the way are being opened. Sweaty now but highly energized from the morning's routine, we happily walk back home, taking the same route we had taken before.

As we walk by our store, we see that it is also opened already. *A-kuh* is already seated on his usual chair at the side entrance. Tino can be seen buffing the floor or cleaning the glass windows . Tirong is also there tending to his chores. We stop by to chat a bit with *A-kuh*. He is always happy to see us.

We could also see the vendors along the side of the store prepping up their wares of cigarettes, lighters, combs, nail clippers, etc. The vendors on this side of the store actually come from one extended family. They just laid claim to the space which is actually a sidewalk. Their other stall sells fried *banana cue*. They have sacks of plantain bananas which they peel then deep fry in a wok filled with cooking oil. Once these have browned, they sprinkle brown sugar all over the bananas. This turns into a golden caramelized color. Then they put two pieces of the cooked banana into a barbecue stick. These finished *banana cue* sticks are then placed in a deep basin where they sell for around twenty centavos per stick.

By the time we get home, Mama is sweating profusely and gets the fan to vigorously fan herself. Papa has already come down for the morning. He could be seen reading the Chinese newspaper which is delivered daily to our house. As usual, his feet are up on a chair that he placed across him in the sofa. In a while, the man who delivers carabao milk also shows up at the door. He carries a wooden pole on two ends of which hang the baskets carrying the milk bottles he delivers house to house. Pa drinks one bottle of this fresh milk every day together with four pieces of soft boiled eggs for his breakfast. Mama would put four fresh eggs in a big bowl, boil water in the kettle and pour the boiling water into the bowl of eggs. She then covers it up, and allows the boiled water to cook the eggs. When Papa is ready to eat his breakfast, he would crack open the egg on the top end, then peel a little of the shell, put in a pinch of rock salt, and sip the soft boiled egg. This was his routine breakfast for as long as we were growing up.

My other brothers and sisters would also be up by this time. We have a big paper bag of hot *pandesal* on the table. Often, Mama has cooked fried eggs or cocktail hotdogs, or sardines to go along with the bread. Sometimes, we would have leftover viands from last night's supper to go with the bread or fried rice. We also have coffee for our breakfast.

Some days Mama would bring home some native delicacies like *puto* or *bibingka* (rice cakes) from the market. And we would happily eat these as well. Mama sits down beside Papa and relaxes for a while, all the time fanning herself with the native round bamboo fan which is her constant companion. They would talk for a while after which Ma would eat her breakfast before starting to cook.

# Helping Ma in the Kitchen

"Lydia! You can start making the ingredients for *toyoma* (pork in soy sauce) now," said Mama. "Okay!" I cheerfully replied. I was looking forward to a morning of assisting Ma in the kitchen. By this time, I already knew the basic ingredients that go into her favorite dishes like *adobo*, *toyoma*, sauted veggies, *pancit*, fried fish, etc. For *toyoma* I would be needing crushed garlic with skin on and soy sauce and of course, pork cubes. I looked at the big chunk of frozen meat which Mama had taken out of the freezer earlier in the morning to thaw. Cleaver in hand, I proceeded to first cut the big meat into two. Then I sliced off the skin and put it aside. With the remaining meat, I cut bite size cubes which had both fat and lean meat. It wasn't exactly cubed but more of rectangular bite sized portions. I then prepared the garlic which for this dish doesn't need to be chopped, but merely pounded flat and with its skin on. It's almost nine o'clock in the morning. Papa is almost finished with his morning newspapers. Mama has just finished having her coffee and breakfast.

I learned a lot of kitchen skills from my mom. Not only did Mama teach me how to cook, but she also made sure I learned how to clean and prepare the various meats that went into cooking. At that time, we had no dressed chicken or filleted fish. Mama bought live chicken and fresh fish complete with scales and gills. Because of this, it was necessary that one knows how to slaughter the chicken and clean the fish. Mama would have a bowl filled with thin raw rice vermicelli (*misua* as we called it). She would squat on the floor and holding the chicken with its feet under her arm and holding the beak with one hand, she would proceed to slit its throat with a sharp knife. Blood would start gushing down the neck of the chicken and trickle straight down to the bowl underneath. The poor chicken would be kicking and squawking all the time but Mama was firm in her resolve. She would wait until the shudders go from violent to become spurts and totally die down as the last of the blood is squeezed out. Chicken blood tasted real good fried or stewed. Afterwards, Mama would pour boiling water over the dead chicken and then begin pulling off the feathers, making sure that the remaining skin of the chicken is almost smooth before she stops. Then she would get her cleaver and cut off the head and the neck after which she would pull out the innards and all the gunk saving only the heart, the liver, the gizzards, and throw out the rest of the intestines. Then she would cut the chicken into bite size portions, making sure she cuts off thru the cartilage so that she doesn't break the bones. Writing this down now sure makes my skin crawl, because it seems so cruel. But back then, it was an accepted practice. That was the only way you could eat your chicken. Although my mom used to joke afterwards that having slaughtered so many chickens herself, she has no doubt they would all come to meet her when she gets over to the next life.

After Ma finishes cutting up the chicken, she would give them over to me. I would first rub the cut parts with salt, and then taking them one piece at a time, wash them under running water. Ma would remind me to be sure and clean off the slime which is found between the chicken skin and meat. Now, the chicken is ready to be cooked.

Cleaning up fish is another messy business. After you have un-wrapped the fish from the paper cover, you put it in a basin. If there are scales, you use a cleaver to take those off. You just pass the cleaver along the surface and the scales will come off as you scrape. Then, you cut off the gills and pull the innards through the opening in the mouth. Sometimes, it is necessary to make a slit in this opening to totally remove the intestines. After washing the fish in tap water, I would rub it with rock salt. I get the rock salt from the big clay jar that sits on the kitchen table. This black jar has a hole on top just big enough for one hand to dip into it for the needed salt. Mama buys rock salt from a traveling vendor. Yes, rock salt was sold on the street with the vendor peddling it on foot as he goes from one neighborhood to another. We buy it by the kilo and stock it in the jar. Mama believes that one should always have salt in the house for good feng shui. And if one were to move, the first items one needs to bring to the new house would be rice and salt. It is a rule of thumb that Filipinos can survive during times of extreme poverty by subsisting just on rice and salt. One such period I remember was during the time of Pres. Carlos Garcia, when the supply of rice became dangerously low and we would buy rice mixed with corn. Filipinos are rice eaters and I myself cannot imagine going without rice for extended periods of time. The cooked rice which was mixed with corn actually tasted good.

"Lydia! Come here quick! Scratch the back of my neck. I think there is an ant crawling there!" Mama shouts. I would laughingly oblige. This happens often when Mama is in the midst of mashing the ground meat and onions for a meatball recipe or some such instances when both her hands are messy. I loved to spend my time just watching her cook. And I would clean up as she finishes one dish after another. Since the wok is of heavy iron and the stove is a kerosene burning type, high heat really contributed to the truly delicious dishes that came out of it. As the viands are cooked one after the other, Ma would put the dish inside a screened wooden cabinet by the side of the stove where she also keeps the clean bowls and plates.

As the clock ticks, and the hour for the arrival of the famished people from the family store and the other children arrive for the noonday meal, Mama's sweat and adrenalin would also rise correspondingly. And many a time, I would hear Ma asking where the ladle or the wok is. "I just finished washing and storing it" goes my quick reply. At which, Mama would scold me "Why did you wash it already, I still need to use it". "Get out of here! You are always in a hurry to finish up! Go! Go!" Thus, goes our hilarious banter. This is Aling Sion, always quick to lose her temper, but knowing my mom, she is just being herself. And I totally love her. Instead of scaring me, it just humors me.

For many years, we didn't own a refrigerator. It was much later when I was already in high school that Pa brought home a refrigerator. I guess that was why Mama had to go to the market every day. You couldn't store raw meats or fish. The good thing about it was we always had fresh food. Meat tasted so good because it was always fresh. Just washing it and steaming it gives off a very pleasant and appetizing aroma. And we were always eating fruits and vegetables in season. That was an essential by product of those times. When you eat, you could be sure you were really being nourished. Marketing, preparing, and cooking were an essential part of our family life. And as Papa loves to quip, "Eating is prosperity."

# Cooking Mama's Yummy Bagoong

One of Mama's most popular dishes was "*bagoong*". This is super tiny shrimp that has been fermented in salt and then cooked with pork fat, garlic, and vinegar. The process of preparing it from scratch is quite tedious. People nowadays can buy it in bottles off the shelf in supermarkets. But back then, we had the luxury of eating home cooked *bagoong* done in the unique way that only Aling Sion can muster.

Mama buys the tiny shrimps in the wet market. She looks for a particular quality of shrimps which she deems best for making into *bagoong*. Needless to say, it has to be really fresh. When she chances upon the exact variety in the market, she buys almost a kilo or two of it. Once finished, this comes up to a big bowl of cooked *bagoong*.

Upon coming home, she would put the batch of shrimp in a big basin careful not to wet it, as this would spoil the pickling process. Then she would proceed to pick out the small pebbles and shells in the pile of shrimps.

After making sure that there are no more unwanted objects in the shrimp, Mama would rub it with rock salt. She uses a lot of salt for this, easily a cup. Then she would mash it with her fingers. She would rub in the salt and massage the mixture with her bare hand for around ten minutes or so until the whole thing reaches a slightly thick, pasty consistency. After this, she would get a clean, dry bottle, put the mixture in and then gently screw the bottle shot. It would then be placed on an upper shelf and not touched or opened for around three days, letting the shrimp soak in the salt and enter a fermenting phase. My mom claims that if your hands are "rotten" as she terms it, you would never be able to come up with a good *bagoong*.

After the three days are up, Ma would unscrew the bottle. The shrimp is now pasty in texture and almost lavender in color. It is now ready for the wok. Mama sautes pork fat cut into thin small strips until the oil oozes out and the pork strips turn crunchy. She then adds about a cup of finely minced garlic until it turns deliciously aromatic and golden brown. This is just about the right time to pour in the fermented shrimp. She stirs the shrimp slowly allowing it to absorb the hot oil from the pork fat. Ma then pours in white vinegar, around a cup or two of it. The vinegar neutralizes the saltiness of the paste. In the meantime, Ma would continue to move the whole thing around, letting it absorb the vinegar, the fat and the garlic, until the mixture dries up a bit. Ma is almost gentle in her movements and does the swirling with slow, gentle strokes. Then taking a small teaspoon, she would taste the *bagoong* and usually she would decide to add on more cooking oil and vinegar, taking care to continue stirring it. Gradually the color of the shrimp paste takes on a shiny brownish tinge with a smattering of crunchy bits of toasted pork fat. And like a symphony, the aroma also builds up in crescendo. All in all, the whole cooking process alone could easily take up thirty minutes or more. As the aroma of the *bagoong* fill up the house, I can imagine those within smelling distance quietly whispering "What a heavenly aroma". And indeed it is truly heavenly and we were sure to have a truly hearty meal afterwards. Ma usually paired the *bagoong* with *kare kare* (peanut meat stew). Sometimes we would just put in mashed fresh tomatoes and eat it with fried fish and rice.

It was a pity Papa never tasted Mama's *bagoong* specialty. If there was one thing Papa never touched, it was *patis* (fish sauce) and *bagoong*. Being Chinese, Papa takes soy sauce instead of *bagoong* or *patis* for condiments. But when Mama passed away, I noticed that Pa developed a liking for the *bagoong* that later became available in the supermarkets. They came in bottles and had different brands like Barrio Fiesta. That must have been Pa's own way of remembering Ma in the dishes that she used to whip up so expertly. Although these store bought condiments never came up to par with Mama's version.

# Mama's Fish Bolabola

The fish ball recipe of Ma is among the many top favorites in our family. However, like so many of her other popular dishes, this is another recipe that requires skill and patience. It goes without saying that the type of fish that goes into the making of this dish is not one that is available every day. On the days that she is able to buy *bitbit*, a type of milkfish that is long and thin compared to the regular *bangus* as we call it, Ma would brace herself for a whole morning of preparation to cook her *bola bola* soup.

Upon coming home from the market, Ma would instruct the maid to clean the fish. She usually buys around three kilos of *bitbit* for her recipe. The maid would take care of cleaning, gutting, scaling, and cutting the fish lengthwise and then scooping out the flesh. As she scrapes the flesh out, quite a bit of fish bones get mixed in with the scooped flesh. After all the fish have been treated thus, the maid throws away the bones and the skin, and turns over the finished product to Mama.

Before tackling the fish though, Ma would first prepare her ingredients: half cup of finely minced garlic, a big bowl of chopped pork fat, chopped spring onion, ginger chopped roughly and soaked in a glass of tap water, almost a half cup of rock salt, and cornstarch. When this is done, she is ready.

First, she would run the soaked ginger in a sieve and pour the ginger fluid into the fish. This is done to remove the fishy smell. Then she would begin to mash the fish. Salt is next and as she continues to mash the mixture, she would already be removing the fish bones. This is a tedious task and in a short while, she would put in the pork fat and the minced garlic. One has to be meticulous in removing the bones as a perfectly deboned mixture is essential. Mama keeps a bowl of water on hand to put in the fish bones. All the while she is mashing the mixture and little by little, a sharp chomping sound like a crackle can be heard with this action. That is an indication of the fish's freshness. Again Ma would laughingly remark that "if your hands are rotten, you won't be able to come up with good *bola bola*." She would add in a little more of the ginger fluid as she sees fit. And as fish bones get all cleared out, Ma would start putting in the cornstarch. The mixture would get sticky as this is done, and the crackle would increase. The whole process easily takes up forty five minutes. When this is finished, Ma would sauté some ginger slices and garlic in cooking oil and then fill the casserole with water.

As the broth is boiling, Ma prepares for the next phase. She places a glass of water near her. With her left hand, she forms a ball of the mixture, and with her right hand, she scoops this ball with a spoon and drops it into the boiling water. Expertly she drops the fish balls one by one and for the first few pieces, she would ask me if I am there to get a taste of it. Satisfied with the seasonings, she continues until every piece has been cooked.

For variation, she would put chopped spring onion into the remaining mixture and make big chunks instead of balls. When she is feeling especially creative, she would get a square aluminum pan and pour in the remaining fish mixture, top it with beaten egg and long slices of spring onion. Then she would steam this, and later on, she would cut this into squares for presentation.

Lunch with fish ball soup is always greatly enjoyed. The huge soup bowl is emptied fast and replenished just as fast. Together with steaming hot white rice, the satisfied faces of everybody is enough sign of appreciation for Mama. *A-kuh* would oftentimes continue to tarry at the kitchen after his lunch to talk with Mama, and with a fork in his hand eat some more pieces of the delicious fish balls.

When Papa comes home for his lunch, Ma would add the specially made *bola bola* cut in squares to the soup and add a drop of whiskey to it as she heats it up. And alongside the already tasty soup, Mama would cook an extra dish of Shanghai fried rice especially for Papa.

Later on when we became practicing Catholics, meatless Fridays of the Lenten season turned out to be more celebratory than penitential because Mama would concoct delectable seafood dishes instead of meat dishes for Papa. During such days, deep fried prawns, steamed crabs and other sea food delicacies became the flavor of the day. And not surprisingly my brothers would patiently wait for Papa's turn for lunch to take their meal because they were sure to partake of extra delicious fares as a reward for their patience.

# Mama's Fresh Lumpia

Mrs. Ong's fresh *lumpia* dinner was always eagerly awaited not just by our family but also by Papa's circle of friends. It is a feast that is preceded by at least two days of focused preparation.

It starts with an early afternoon trip to Divisoria, specifically Elcano, which is a drop off point for fresh vegetables coming from different parts of the archipelago. Armed with two or three *bayongs* (native baskets), Mama brings a maid and sometimes the old reliable me in tow. We take a *jeepney* ride which goes straight to Divisoria.

After getting off the *jeepney*, we go on foot until we reach Elcano where we are greeted with an exciting sight of colorful, vibrant, luscious vegetables everywhere. Here, fresh vegetables from all parts of the archipelago find their way. Huge crates of carrots, cabbage, garlic, onions, *singkamas*, *camote*, potatoes, bananas, spring onions, broccoli, cauliflower and more line the streets. People buy in bulk and the prices are super low. I had the impression that the sellers in the many small stores in this area actually lived in them. Women sit on stools beside their wares, fanning themselves and looking unhurried. They tear off slightly discolored outer leaves of cabbages and throw them away. I am dismayed because in my child's eye, I feel they are still good enough to cook. Pretty soon, a thin raggedy boy lugging along a limp discolored sack picks up these pieces of veggies and I am relieved knowing that at least these scraps won't go to waste after all.

Mama haggles her way in buying many kilos of carrots, cabbage, *singkamas*, *sayote*, baguio beans, and lettuce which will all go towards making her fresh *lumpia*. She makes a quick calculation of fifty or more pieces of *tokwa* (firm tofu) that she needs. For this, we hie off to a corner wooden structure which turns out to be the factory where tofu is made. The place is like a steam sauna where tofu pieces are steamed in racks of wooden shelves. The man counts the *tokwa* we need and wraps them up. Mama is pleased because she actually saved quite a sum buying wholesale. Nearby is the *lumpia* wrapper factory. Here lumpia wrapper in various sizes are manufactured. Mama decides to buy a hundred pieces of the wrapper. She adds twenty pieces more. She always chooses the large *lumpia* wrappers . We are delighted to see an abundant supply of cilantro which is a must for delicious *lumpia*. Mama also picks up raw peanuts which she would roast on the wok before grinding it using a big Nescafe bottle which she rolls on top of the peanuts to grind them.

As a bonus, Mama picks up garlic and onions which are so much cheaper over here. After shopping for over two hours, we have more than we could carry. For the trip back home, Mama hails a *caretela*. This is like a *calesa* only it has a fenced space around it and is used for transporting cargo as well as people. We climb up the *caretela* relieved to finally rest our weary feet.

As soon as we arrive home, we take a few minutes to take *merienda* (snacks) and to rest. Then Mama assigns each of us a vegetable to wash, peel, cut, chop, and grate. With so much to peel, we are looking like a marketplace ourselves. Masing shows her skill in chopping and feels pride in chopping with machine like speed. Mama instructs us to grate the carrots to make it finer because Chinese fresh *lumpia* tastes much better the more mushy it is. I always volunteer to do the *tokwa* because it is the easiest to cut and puts less strain on my arms. The cabbage is likewise soft and easier to do although Mama is quick to remind me that I have to cut it as thinly as possible. *Repolyo* as we call it in Manila is loose and airy in its insides unlike cabbage in the states which is thick and much heavier. Mama boils the chicken and the pork belly until they are soft and tender. After the boiled meats are cooled, I cut it in strips. Whole heads of garlic are chopped. The cut ingredients are placed in the rectangular serving bowls, so Mama can see if we have enough of the ingredients. Mama never scrimps in the ingredients she uses in cooking *lumpia*. Tomorrow we will tackle the shrimps. After shelling and deveining the shrimps, I usually cut the shrimp in half by running the cleaver along its back where the black intestine runs and this I also remove. The shells will then be boiled in water to make the shrimp broth. After we are finished with the vegetables, we call it a day.

We store the cut ingredients in the refrigerator. After cooking lunch the following day, Mama starts her lumpia. It is easier today because with all the ingredients ready, it is all just a matter of sautéing and mixing everything. Ma starts by sautéing her garlic, followed by the shrimps, and then the meats. It isn't just a matter, though, of throwing everything into the pan. Mama insists that a good cook shows her mettle by the aroma of her sautéing. Of course high heat is a must, and the dance of the garlic, the shrimp, the meats and *tokwa* prepares the foundation for the parade of vegetables to follow. She likes to fry the *tokwa* until it browns and crisps up before she throws in the rest of the veggies starting with the carrots, *singkamas*, *sayote*, cabbage, baguio beans, and finally the bean sprouts. She adds the broth using both the meat broth and the shrimp broth as she goes along. As the wok fills up, she transfers the mixture to a casserole. There is a lot of mixing all the time. It is essential that the vegetables are properly mixed. With beads of perspiration starting to form on her forehead, Mama continues mixing, adding broth, more vegetable oil, transferring the contents to the casserole, and ultimately, the succession of vegetables undergo the same treatment. At the end of the cooking process, she ends up with two giant cauldrons of cooked fresh *lumpia*.

As dinner time approaches, the table is set with an array of trays containing the *lumpia* wrapper which the maid has painstakingly separated and covered with damp cheesecloth to keep it from drying, and the fresh lettuce which have also been washed and broken into individual leaves. Then the smaller bowls of ground peanuts mixed with white sugar, chopped fresh garlic soaked in water to keep its freshness, cilantro leaves, and the *lumpia* sauce which Mama had made by boiling soy sauce, sugar, and cornstarch mixed with water. The brown sauce is just right, neither runny nor overly thick. The crowning glory of the feast is of course the *lumpia* mixture itself. And to have this, one more task needs to be done, and that is the straining of the liquid from the *lumpia*. Mama has a large colander with a wooden handle unto which the mixture is poured and pressed to squeeze out the liquid.

At around seven thirty in the evening, Papa, *A-kuh*, and Papa's other regular friends arrive at the house to partake of the *lumpia* feast. They take their seats around the table and with a plate in front of them, they wrap their own *lumpia*. To finally savor this dish, one needs to put in a little work of laying first the *lumpia* wrapper on one's plate, scooping the sauce unto the upper portion of the wrapper, then laying the fresh lettuce leaf on the lower half, piling it up with the *lumpia* mixture, topping it with the sweet ground peanut, garlic, cilantro, hot sauce, and finally rolling the wrapper up like a burrito. And as one finally take a bite, heaven!

Papa has his own unique way of wrapping his *lumpia*. He needs two of the large *lumpia* wrapper, and proceeds to pour a huge amount of *lumpia* mixture so that he ends up with a giant *lumpia* which he then eats with relish. His one piece is equivalent to roughly three or four pieces of mine because I usually make mine small. I always enjoyed watching Papa do his *lumpia*. Mama, on the other hand, almost always dislikes wrapping up the *lumpia* for herself. I suppose by this time, she is bone tired from all the cooking and would delegate this task to Linda or me. Everybody in our family enjoys *lumpia* so much that often at the end of the day Papa would announce "*ko ban tsi ban*", meaning let's do it again tomorrow. And Mama agrees. The second time around is easier, because Mama would just add a little more veggies, and using the same leftover broth makes everything so much simpler.

Sometimes with the leftover mixture, we would go one step further and fry the *lumpia* coming up with fried rolls which we dip in vinegar and eat with rice. Fresh or fried, *lumpia* is always an easy favorite. Too bad, this type of fresh *lumpia* can only be found in Manila. It seems to be a virtual unknown abroad. Fortunately, my sisters and I know enough to prepare it in our own homes nowadays.

# A Shortlist of Mama's Everyday Dishes

"Your mom's a great cook" *Lau-um*, an old Chinese neighbor and one of mom's good friends used to remark to me as I visit with and interact with her daughter, Ale. "She comes up with so many new dishes every day. I really admire her cooking abilities." She would comment further. *Lau-um* is a bespectacled thin, tiny old lady with her black hair always in a bun and two small Salonpas strips on both her temples. She lived with her husband, a son and a daughter, and I guess they really didn't cook much because they have lunch and dinner delivered to their house daily. A man carrying a long wooden pole on which hung several sets of aluminum tin packs goes to their house for these deliveries.

Mrs. Ong as my mom is lovingly addressed was known for her mouthwatering dishes. She herself didn't know she had this talent because as she loved to tell me, she didn't know how to cook at all when she first got married. My father who loved to eat and prided himself with knowing the secrets to good cooking must have influenced and honed this talent in her. Pa was a food gourmet and critic if you ever met one. He often chided me when I would help out in the kitchen. According to him, the secret to good tasting food starts with how you cut, chop, dice, or mince your ingredients. Dishes require that the meats and vegetables are cut precisely. This often overlooked prerequisite is an important factor that determines whether the dish you cook will taste good or not. The harmony of the entire dish comes together with the shape and texture, color and aroma of the many different ingredients that go into its making. It is like a symphony orchestra where every single instrument playing in synchronicity determines the quality of the total performance.

Some of the usual daily dishes in our house were *adobo, toyoma, tausima, hongma,* fried fish, *sinigang, pancit, menudo, mechado, dinuguan, kare kare,* meatballs, fish ball soup, fish head soup, pork rib soup, steamed pork, egg custard, minced pork with salted egg, minced pork with black or brown beans, fried chicken, *okoy* or fritters, *adobo* eggplant, *pakbet, monggo guisado, camaron,* oysters and other shellfish cooked a variety of ways sometimes with just boiling water poured over it to slightly cook it. Aside from this, Mama liked to experiment with restaurant dishes she liked, like *sate guma hohun* or *ampalaya con carne.*

*Toyoma* – This is a basic stewed pork dish. The pork is cut into chunky cubes, oftentimes with the skin on. Long rectangular pieces of meat with the skin, fat, and lean meat are cut from the big block of pork that Mama brings home from the market. On the casserole, she puts in the meat, and adds whole cloves of garlic which has been pounded to release the juice. Then, she puts in about two tablespoons of soy sauce. She puts the heat on high and swirls the meat around until the fat is extracted. She does this by putting water a little bit at a time to coax out the juice. After the meat has charred with enough fat extracted, one can smell the slightly burnt aroma of meat and soy sauce and garlic. The burnt bottom of the casserole will by now start to smell good. Then she adds water, allows the mixture to boil, put it down to simmer, and continue cooking until the meat becomes tender and done.

To this basic *toyoma* dish, she sometimes adds hard-boiled eggs just when the dish is almost done. The hard boiled eggs are then incorporated into the meat mixture until it too acquires the brown color of the *toyoma*. Sometimes, shredded pickled radish bought from the Chinese grocer is added, or dried banana blossoms, or fried tofu cut in rectangular pieces. It could be *tokwa* or tofu.

*Adobo* – This popular Filipino dish has many variations depending on the region where it originated. We like Mama's version of it best. For pork *adobo*, she would cut chunks of pork squares. Then she would put this in a casserole, pour in about a third cup of vinegar, minced garlic, tomatoes, and onion, and a little water. She would cook the mixture until it boils. Then she would simmer it until the pork becomes tender. This takes about twenty to thirty minutes. After this, she would get her wok, transfer the mixture into the wok leaving behind the broth. Then, she would brown the pork pieces by adding cooking oil and soy sauce, allowing the pieces to crisp up. When the pork has exuded a nice fried aroma and the color has turned deliciously golden brown, she would pour in the broth of the *adobo* mixture. Soon enough the *adobo* turns into a pinkish color emitted by the combined tomatoes and soy sauce and the frying process. Then, Mama would continue tenderizing the pork by simmering it and allowing the sauce to thicken up as it dries up a bit.

To add extenders to the *adobo dish*, Mama would deep fry pieces of potato wedges and add it when the dish is in the latter period of tenderizing. When the children chance upon these fried potatoes waiting to be added, we don't think twice about gobbling them up. They sure taste better than french fries, although during those times, fast food french fries were still unheard of. This gets Ma all riled up because she needed those potatoes for the dish.

Meatballs – This is one dish all of us relish. When this is her planned menu for the day, Mama would bring a piece of onion with her to the market, so that she could ask the pork vendor to mince the pork meat together with the onion. This is her ingredient for our favorite meatballs. To further prepare the ground meat, she would add in minced garlic, salt and pepper, sugar, and cornstarch to the mixture. Then, she would heat up cooking oil for deep frying in the wok. And as she spoons the ground mixture, she would also be quick enough to scoop up the meatballs as they turn golden brown. We usually eat this with ketchup. And we children always finish it in no time at all.

Pork Rib Soup – This is one dish Mama often served. For this, she buys pork ribs which are not too meaty.

Actually, a lot of the lean meat has been removed and this is mostly just scraps and cheap. The bones are what make it really tasty. For this recipe, Mama would sauté minced garlic, add in the short ribs, add fish sauce, and plenty of water. Then she would boil it and then allow it to simmer until done. Oftentimes, she adds radish cut in chunks. We always had soup as part of the balanced meal Mama serves.

*Picadillo* – This is another soup dish. Mama sautés garlic, onion, and tomatoes, cubed potatoes, and ground beef. Then she puts in water and once it has boiled, adds in soy sauce and simmers the whole thing until it is cooked. Danny and I used to love to get the potatoes, mash it with our fork and put in *patis* or fish sauce. Nice!

*Dinuguan* – This uniquely Filipino dish is a favorite in our house. After sautéing garlic, onions, tomatoes, and ground pork, Mama would pour in the chunks of pig blood. Then she would put in white vinegar and allow it to come to a boil. To add in some kick, she would put two or three pieces of green jalapeno peppers, salt and white ground pepper. Eating *dinuguan* with hot white rice is always refreshing. Some people like to eat their *dinuguan* with *puto* (rice cakes).

*Adobong Pusit* – When the squid is large and fat, Mama likes to just steam it with slivers of ginger. Otherwise, when the squid is small, she cooks it into *adobong pusit*. She would leave the black pouch on its head and instead of removing it, she would just rinse it together with the rest of the squid. She would remove the hard round thing on top of its head and cut the body into round slices. After sautéing ginger, tomatoes and onions, she would put in the squid, tentacles and all. As the black ink spreads out, Mama would put in vinegar and salt and pepper. She would also add in some jalapeno peppers to make it spicy. The ink renders a thickness to the sauce and if it is deeply black, adding in a little more oil gives it a shiny finish. Eaten with white rice and *patis*, this makes a delightful meal.

*Okoy* – This is a fritter dish. For this, Mama mixes sweet potatoes cut in thin strips and bean sprouts in a big basin. She adds in flour and achuete water until a thick enough consistency is formed. On a side plate, she has tofu cut into thin rectangular pieces and raw shrimps with the nose tips cut off. She then prepares the wok for deep frying. When the oil is hot enough, Mama would spoon the batter into a small round saucer, top it with pieces of tofu and shrimps, then drops it slowly into the hot oil. She would fry as many pieces as the wok could hold. After it has turned golden brown, she would cook the other side of the fritter. And when the fritters are done, she lines them up in a native basket colander. She always cooked a big batch of them and I always dreaded having to finish cooking the batch if she chanced upon me not doing anything.

*Pok Kwe* – This is chicken braised in whiskey. Mama marinates the chicken pieces in soy sauce for about an hour or so. Then she sautés about two or three tablespoons of fine strips of ginger in cooking oil until it turns brown and aromatic but not burnt. Then she puts in the chicken plus its marinade, adds a little water and continue cooking until the chicken becomes tender and the water is reduced. With the pan in high heat, she pours a tablespoon or two of whiskey. By this time, the chicken has turned golden brown and slightly crispy. Mama allows the alcohol to evaporate leaving the cooked chicken in its bed of shiny oil, crunchy with a hint of gelatin in its skin. I remember Mama cooked a whole platter of this dish for me when I gave birth and she had me finish it all by myself in order to enable me to regain my strength from childbirth.

*Pancit* – Mama cooked *pancit* or noodles every time there is a birthday in the family. These could be one of any type of Chinese dried noodles, *sotanghon, bihon, canton, miki,* or *misua*. Her *pancit* dishes always taste good because she puts in a good quantity of fine ingredients in them like, fresh shrimps, pork fat, lean meat, Chinese dried mushrooms, and vegetables like cabbage, onion, garlic, spring onions, or cilantro. First off, she would fry the sliced pork fat until its oil comes out. Then she would put in a tablespoon or two of white sugar until it caramelizes after which she sautes the garlic, onion, shrimp and pork. The added sugar gives it a pinkish color. When this is done, she puts in the shredded cabbage. Next, she would pour in the shrimp broth which she does by boiling the shrimp heads and shells in water and then straining the broth. While waiting for the mixture to boil, she would put in soy sauce, salt, and pepper. She always makes sure that the broth is just enough for the quantity of pancit she was cooking. Too much or too little broth will make the dish either soggy or overly dry. When the mixture boils, she puts in the noodles, and makes sure everything is thoroughly mixed. Oftentimes, she sets aside a part of the condiments of shrimps and pork to use as topping. Then she rounds it off by sprinkling spring onions on top.

These are but some of the many, many dishes of my mom. She does her cooking without using any fixed measurements. She always just follows her gut when putting in the seasonings in her dishes. She believes that a good cook does not rely on exact measurements but on her instincts. This in turn requires years of experience to develop. The basic seasonings she uses are the simple soy sauce, vinegar, salt, sugar, and pepper. A trick she taught me when one happens to put too much salt in a dish that is still in the process of cooking is to add potatoes to the mixture. Potatoes absorb salt and will reduce the saltiness of the dish. Sometimes when the meat, especially beef, happens to be tough and is taking too long to cook, she would put in a clean piece of broken ceramic saucer in the pot. She swears on its effectiveness as a tenderizer.

For many years after I got married and did my own cooking, I would always think of how Mama cooked this and that, and I got stuck into thinking it couldn't be done any other way. It took me a long time to develop the courage to experiment with ingredients and espouse a think the taste attitude towards cooking. I was finally able to free myself from this self imposed limitation. It is no surprise that all of us brothers and sisters know how to cook. Oftentimes, we try to replicate the dishes of Mama and we try in this way to bring back her legacy in our own kitchens and households.

# School – Here We Come

"Wake up!! Wake up!! Wake up!!" It's six o'clock and Mama could be heard rousing us for school. Mama has been awake since five o'clock during which time she has managed not only to finish her bathroom routines but has also cooked breakfast and prepared the coffee for the children and tea for Papa. Most days she wakes up earlier than the house helps, who upon waking up would proceed to sweep and scrub the living room floor.

The children would come down one by one and take turns using the one bathroom of the house. With around seven of us going to school at the same time, one can imagine how much of a feat this daily morning ritual could be. It was not uncommon to hear yelling and knocking on the toilet door to get it over and done with because there are others who needed to use the bathroom. Meanwhile, I was the one who was almost always tasked to fix the seven cups of coffee for the brood. Yes, for the longest time there were seven of us attending elementary school and we had to leave the house no later than seven o'clock. Every morning, Ma would boil water in the coffee casserole, put in around two tablespoons of coffee grounds and come up with brewed coffee weak enough for us children to drink.

Meantime, the maid has opened the wooden door letting in the first rays of the sun. Then she goes to the store next door to buy our bread. Easily she would have bought at least twenty pieces of *pandesal* (buns). *Pandesal* in Manila always tasted good even without filling because we usually buy it right off the grill when it was still piping hot and smelled really good. To this day, I have yet to taste bread that could beat the texture and taste of old Manila's hot *pandesal*. Always crisp and brown on the outside and airy on the inside, one could eat *pandesal* as is without needing to put anything inside to make it more palatable. Often, poor laborers would just order a cup of weak coffee from the *sari-sari* store and two pieces of *pandesal* which they dip into the hot coffee for a morning meal or an afternoon snack. For breakfast, Mama would have fried eggs and sardines on the table. Or else, leftover pork *adobo* was heated to fill the bread. We bring with us two pieces of *pandesal* each for our midmorning snack in school. I still remember the cocktail hotdogs that Mama sometimes prepared. Small as they already are, these hotdogs are further cut into four pieces each for the buns. We ate well, but we were also frugal, knowing all the time that whatever we have should be able to go around so that all could eat.

After everyone has eaten and gotten dressed, we would file out before Mama, who seated on her chair at the breakfast table, would give us each our *baon* (pocket money) of ten centavos. To the eldest of the brood, she entrusts the transport fare of 30 centavos going and 40 centavos coming home. We always came home for lunch because our classes in the afternoon start at around 1:30 for the Chinese lessons.

We often took the *calesa* going to school. A *calesa* was a horse drawn carriage with a seat in front for the driver and a bench at the back that could comfortably seat three people. Our regular position riding this was usually one child at the driver's seat with the driver crouching at the side so he could direct the horse. At the back there would be three seated properly with another three on their laps. Together with our schoolbags, we are indeed a heavy burden for the poor horse.

Sometimes we would decide to just take a taxi in the morning since traffic was still light and it would give us all a more comfortable ride. Unfortunately, we sometimes met with traffic. During such times, we would watch the taximeter with baited breaths as it ticked down the fare. It must have been extremely amusing for the driver to see and feel seven pairs of anxious eyes intently focused on his meter. As soon as it hits THIRTY CENTAVOS, we would shout in unison "Stop! We're getting down now." And we all get off relieved to just walk the remainder of the way. These common plights have managed to create a bond among us children which we managed to keep well until we have each grown up and had families of our own.

But all through our stay at St. Stephen's, the *calesa* remained our favorite mode of transport. Of course it was almost always difficult to get a ride for the brood simply because there were so many of us who needed to squeeze in for the small amount of space. And there were times when the poor horse would literally fall down because of the sheer weight on its back. I well remember two of my brothers who were not as thick faced as the rest of us girls. Danny and Bobby developed a habit of just opting out of the haggling part when it comes time to get a ride. This was during lunch break when demand for a *calesa* ride was always greater than its supply. The two of them would hide out in a store while I bargain with the driver for a fare. As soon as a deal is reached, we would eagerly climb up the *calesa*. And from nowhere Danny and Bobby would rush to join us, prompting the driver to ask just how many we are. Every so often, after hearing that we were seven in all, the driver would back out of the deal, and down we go to try our luck once again.

At other times when the weather is bad and the rain is pouring, the boys would manfully declare that they have decided to just walk home to make it easier for us girls to get a ride. But they would at the same time leave their schoolbags behind. And oftentimes to our dismay, we find we couldn't get a ride ourselves. Swearing never again to be taken for a ride by our brothers, we wade home in flooded streets with the extra schoolbags.

Funny that one of my clearest memories of St. Stephen's was the smell of horse shit outside the school gates. True, among the more popular modes of transport in the 1960's was the *calesa*. They plied the streets of Chinatown and Magdalena which was where our school was located. The *calesa* is more expensive than the jeepney, but cheaper than a taxi. For a fixed fee which is agreed upon before boarding, one could travel several kilometers at the speed of a horse trot. We usually haggle for the price, and would take a *calesa* to go home for lunch.

My elementary days spent at St. Stephen's High School in Magdalena Street were happy, challenging, and very enjoyable. All my brothers and sisters and I completed elementary education at this school. At that time, it was ranked among the best schools in the Philippines. It was founded by American Episcopalian missionaries. I remember our elementary principal was Ms. Jansen, a very tall amiable American. The principal for high school was Ms. Bolderston, also a white American, dignified and stern looking. I remember that the two of them lived in a small wooden house situated within the school compound. It had its own small garden. The school also had different principals for the Chinese elementary and high school departments. Our Chinese principal was very strict and a disciplinarian. With her short cropped hair and simple blouse and skirt outfit, she projects an image of a stern schoolmaster who will not tolerate misbehavior of any sort. She speaks with short and curt sentences, and one can imagine the terror of any student who is unfortunate enough to be called to her office.

We started schooling at the age of seven. Our uniform then was the usual white polo shirt and khaki pants for the boys, and for the girls, white polo shirt and purple colored skirt with straps. We had a big cemented open field where we held our physical education classes. It also doubled as a basketball court. There were two wooden structures which housed the school offices, classrooms, and library. At the corner beside the principal's house was the auditorium where prayer services and school programs were held. Underneath this structure was the school canteen. My mom always gave us sandwiches for snack and I used to spend the ten centavos pocket money for soft drinks.

Upon arriving, I would bring my school bag to my classroom and leave it there. At the stroke of seven thirty, the bell would ring signaling the start of classes. All the children would assemble on the school grounds in their respective areas according to class and section. After which we would have the flag ceremony. Then, everyone would file in line to go to their respective classrooms. We learned order, discipline, and punctuality early on.

As kindergarteners, we were given milk in aluminum tin cups and cookies for our mid-morning snack. I remember that the teacher would ask us to lay our hands on the table each morning to inspect our fingernails. We were seated two per bench. Colors and shapes were among the first lessons of the children. Writing was also a systematic process. I remember the pad paper where we first learned to write our ABC's. The lines for the capital letters and the small letters were strictly followed as the teacher painstakingly guided us towards writing first in block letters and much later in free style. We had drawing pads where we learned colors and lines and shapes. I remember having to draw the same circular strokes in a whole sheet of paper over and over again. In our Chinese classes, we were taught how to use the Chinese brush and ink to write Chinese characters. Much discipline was required to do Chinese calligraphy. Writing big strokes using thicker brushes was drilled into us by filling up whole sheets of paper with big square boxes for large prints and smaller brushes were used in writing the smaller almost freehand equivalent strokes on sheets of paper with tiny square boxes. Weekend assignments regularly included filling in whole sheets of paper in Chinese calligraphy for submission on Mondays. We also had music classes where we learned to sing and for exams, we were required to go in front of the class individually and sing the learned song. As we entered higher grades, the school held regular declamation contests and presentations of dances, skits, and other pageants. It always made me feel good to be chosen to join these programs and contests. Award ceremonies for honor students were held after every semester where parents were invited.

Recess was of course my favorite period. Taking our sandwiches, we would hurry up to get our preferred spaces in the school grounds to play jump rope, tag or whatever. We were usually in groups of threes and fours. It was always a thrill to play alongside a group of boys whom we had crushes on. Our school was coed, and growing up was a happy period for us. We enjoyed the usual games and camaraderie of young children.

Since it was a Chinese school, almost all my classmates were Chinese majority of whom belonged to the middle and upper middle income class. We spoke in Hokkien. Our

Chinese lessons were held in Mandarin. So in effect we were learning four languages at the same time, Filipino, English, Hokkien, and Mandarin. In high school, Spanish was a required course so that added a fifth to our language skills. Sometimes, though, I felt slightly out of place, mainly because I knew that my mandarin had a Filipino twang to it. My family was of mixed parentage (mestizo), and I was aware I didn't sound as Chinese as the other students. In school we had to have two names, an English name and a Chinese name. My brothers had real Chinese names different from their English names. But for us girls, my Pa preferred to give us Chinese names which were just a phonetic translation of our English names. And I felt that my name sounded awkward in Chinese. Ly-Ja in fookien and Ly-Re in mandarin. That is why first day of classes was always an anxious time for me, because I needed to hear the teacher say it. I always felt it was out of place. Otherwise, I enjoyed my school days immensely. I loved to learn and I developed good friends over the years.

School was highly organized then. We were grouped according to sections, with A being the highest. Being in the A section had its perks. My classmates were regularly high achievers and very seldom did the teacher need to deal with cheating during exams. There was an equal ratio of boys to girls per classroom of around 35 to 40 students. I remember having two classmates with disabilities. Both of them had polio although one uses steel braces while the other used wooden crutches. It didn't matter one bit to us though. There was no discrimination at all, so long as we were doing well in our studies. We had another classmate, a boy, who used to bring a large tube of plastic balloon every day. I could hardly afford to buy the very small tubes. These tubes came with a straw which we used to blow the paste into a balloon. This rich boy would use at most a half of the tube and throw the remaining half into the wastebasket. He often casually remarked that his dad was so rich he needed to waste some of that money. Another friend of mine makes it a habit to give me a piece of imported chocolate every day. I figured I probably don't want to be rich when I grow up.

During recess, I almost always noticed a boy with his mom. They would be seated in the cemented bench. He was quite big so he sweated a lot. His mom would change his shirt first and then would bring out his snack. Wow!! He always had a lot of *siomai* (dumplings) for his midmorning snack. I envied him his food. But I was quite content with my own sandwiches from home and soft drinks. I sometimes liked to buy fried bananas from the school canteen. I also bought pad paper and pencils from the school supplies in school. We had to use paper and notebooks with the school logo. I remember at that young age, I would factor in that expense with my daily allowance instead of asking for extra money. I was aware that I had to be frugal because we weren't rich and had to make do with what we could afford.

We go home for lunch and return in the afternoon for our Chinese classes. Our school bags for the morning English sessions were heavy and bulky. We leave these at home and then go back with lighter bags for the afternoon sessions. At times, Mama would fetch us in the afternoon.

These always made our day because we were sure to have some yummy snacks along the way. She would at times buy fresh *lumpia* from Ha Yuan, an eatery very close to the school which sold authentic fresh Chinese lumpia. We could never afford to buy these ourselves with our daily allowances. At times, when Ma preferred to walk home, we would occasionally stop by an ice cream store and she would buy each of us a popsicle. Once in a while Mama would bring the boys for a haircut. The barbershop was within walking distance from school and also near my grandmother's house. While at the barbershop, there was a stand that sold chicken porridge. For around ten centavos, we could each buy a bowl of hot porridge to tide us over until dinner. Sometimes we would drop by my grandma's house before finally taking a jeepney home.

I have always been nearsighted. But this did not prevent me from developing a voracious appetite for reading. St. Stephen's where we all went to school for our elementary developed this love for reading. We had a subject where we were required to read from a booklet which the teacher kept in the faculty room. When the time comes for the subject, the class officer would bring this stack of booklets to the classroom. There were two sets of booklets for each student. The teacher starts out by requiring us to read from the first. It was usually a short story or an essay. This is a timed exercise. After which, the booklets are collected and given back to the teacher. The second set of booklets is then distributed to the students. This contains the questions which pertain to the article we have just read. We need to answer all the questions which put to test the level of our reading comprehension. I believe it is an excellent way to train our reading skills and foster a love for reading. We were also required to read a book every week or so, and to submit a summary report of the book. I enjoyed this so much that I got really good at it. I also liked reading my lessons aloud at home while making my homework. I can imagine my siblings probably disliking this practice. Looking back I am sure it must have been irritating to hear somebody read aloud especially when you are studying yourself. But I guess I must have done well, because I remember my teacher assigning me to coach my classmates who didn't do well in their reading.

Mathematics was another subject our school taught well. It was a known fact that our class in Chinese was always advanced in its math subject compared to our English class. We had our English classes in the morning and Chinese classes in the afternoon. We might be in the same grade level in our English and Chinese classes, but our Chinese math subject was always a level higher than our English math. I remember the training process our teacher used in teaching us the math equations was to get two students at a time in front of the class. These two would beat each other in answering the equations which the teacher would fire at them. No pen and paper were allowed. For example, "20 plus six". The two students would race each other for the correct answer. With the answer "26", the teacher would follow it up with "multiplied by 10". Again the answer. After which the teacher would say "divided by 2". The answer again. This goes on and leads to more complex equations. This made learning both fun and effective. Aside from accuracy, speed was a premium. I believe the one real advantage of Chinese math was the verbal expressions that went with it. For a simple "1 plus 1 equals 2" in English, the Chinese equivalent was "1...1...2". Six syllables in English equals just three in Chinese for the same equation.

Our school had both Filipino and Chinese teachers. A lot of its students came from comfortable economic backgrounds. Many were children of Chinese store owners in Avenida Rizal and Chinatown. Majority were pure Chinese. Although many were also from Filipino-Chinese families like ourselves. My mother was a Filipino. My father was Chinese. That made us "mestizos" or mixed blood. I think we had the best of both worlds. We were not limited by the strictures of either culture. I never felt shackled by the strictly old world traditions and mindset of the pure Chinese. Nor were we tied down to the unrealistic superstitions of the pure Filipinos. I guess this nurtured a kind of flexibility in our mindsets and approach to life and living. The only thing my parents were uncompromising on was our commitment to our studies. They made sure we understood and realized the seriousness of study and uprightness. We needed to study and study well.

It was in elementary that I realized first hand that effort and enthusiasm plus a modest amount of brains and conscientiousness bring about recognition and reward. Year after year of elementary saw me coming up with first honor awards which meant a gift certificate redeemable from the school department of school supplies. Papa who was my constant companion to these events shared this honors with me not only within the school but also among his countrymen of the same family name. The Ong Association sees to it that all honor students bearing the family name Ong get together once a year to receive cash awards from the organization. I enjoy the generous spread of dimsum dishes that always capped such celebrations.

I learned early on to be responsible for my siblings, and this was especially during my elementary years. I distinctly remember that this started when my twin sisters Espee and Carol started kindergarten. Nursery schools were unheard of then, so kindergarten started when one reached the age of seven. This was usually the first time that children get separated from home for a fairly extended period of time every day. I must have been in grade four when the twins first started school.

The start of the day was marked by a flag ceremony in the quadrangle where all the students are lined up in their respective classes. By seven thirty, we would be properly lined up for the brief flag ceremony and the singing of the national anthem after which everyone would start walking in file towards their respective classrooms. Because they were twins, Espee and Carol were in the same class. As the bell rings for the line up to begin, I was surprised to see my sisters rushing to me in tears. They wanted to go home because their tummies ached. At first I didn't know what to do. Then quick thinking gave me a plan. I would bring the two of them on foot to my uncle *A-kuh's* house which was two blocks away. I was certain he was still home, preparing to go to the store in a few minutes. I would leave the two of them with him. The store was just near our house and that would solve the problem. Yes!! That was an excellent idea. And it worked. I got them off my hands and I was able to go back to my classroom. This ritual repeated itself for several days until Espee and Carol got adjusted.

This same predicament happened again with Bobby, my brother who was younger than the twins. He also took a while before he could adjust to school. But he didn't ask me to bring him home. He merely stayed with me until the bell rang for start of classes. I would walk with him around the school grounds. This was around the time when I was grappling with my own anxiety regarding a dreaded teacher in Chinese geography. I had gotten a low mark in our first test and couldn't get rid of my fear of him. Walking with Bobby helped me until I regained my confidence by studying that subject extra hard and eventually getting high marks in it. It was usual practice then for teachers to spank the palms of students who failed in exams and this really anted up the fear of failing.

One unfortunate incident during our elementary years was when Carol fell off the *calesa* we were riding to school one morning. As was our usual routine, we hailed a *calesa* after walking the stretch of Republic Supermarket and were able to get a ride. We were already within the vicinity of the school when the horse suddenly fell and unfortunately, Carol slipped and fell hard on the pavement. She was so tiny and frail. We all gasped in terror. We felt utterly helpless seeing her. She was stunned and couldn't move her right arm. A Chinese man who lived nearby saw what happened. And without a moment's hesitation, he offered to bring us home in his car. Papa was at home reading the newspaper when we arrived. Immediately, he decided to take Carol to a Chinese chiropractor who had a clinic near our school. Instead of putting a cement cast, the doctor bound her arm in popsicle sticks with a Chinese liniment to immobilize it. The healing took several months and required that Carol stay home from school for the rest of the school year which probably accounted for why she was behind Espee in studies. But the arm healed quite nicely, and Carol was good as new again.

Once in a while, Papa had to go to the principal's office for his children's misdemeanor. Bobby often got the ire of his teacher because he was exceedingly stubborn. And many times, he refused to answer when asked to explain himself. He just kept mum and this infuriates his teacher all the more. But even with Papa there, he remained the way he was.

The one instant I remembered Linda being called to the principal's office was when she was caught fighting with a boy classmate. We had to wait for Linda in the principal's office. I don't know why the principal asked my brother Eddie who started the fight. To our utter dismay Eddie said "Linda started it". We couldn't stop ribbing him after this.

When I was in grade six English and freshman high school in Chinese, I found myself in a dilemma. I had just had my First Communion and was trying to go to regular

Confession. Not knowing what to confess, I decided to tell the priest that I was regularly attending Protestant services in our school. I was dumbfounded when the priest refused to give me absolution unless I promise never to attend those services again. I went out of the confessional deeply troubled. How could I escape attending the assemblies as we call them when they were part of the school curriculum. It was an official class for both English and Chinese classes. I must have stayed in the church for quite a while. After a long while, I went back to the confessional and promised I would not attend the school assemblies again. This was almost a month before the end of classes for the school year. I didn't know how I would do it but I was determined to keep my word.

Assembly for English class was first period on Monday mornings while assembly for the Chinese class was the last period on Friday afternoons. By this time I was already going to school by myself in the morning, and going home by myself in the afternoon. I decided that on Monday mornings, I would leave the house at the same time but wouldn't go directly to school but instead while away the time at a small Catholic chapel near our school. So I was always one period late for classes and by the time I arrive, my classmates would have already returned from assembly. For the Chinese class assembly, an added problem was that being the class president I had to lead the line of the class as we transfer from our classroom to the chapel. What I did was to quietly slip off the line before reaching the chapel. Then I would hide out in the library or the comfort room until the bell rings for end of classes. I remember one time when I asked to be allowed to go home feigning tummy ache. In my mind I could imagine the principal calling me to the office to explain. I decided I would just tell the truth that my religion forbids me to attend the services of a different religion. I figured that being reasonable people, they would understand. Even then I was prepared to face whatever consequences that would bring. But I didn't tell anyone, not even my parents about this. Fortunately, the dreaded call to the principal's office never happened. I eventually persuaded Papa to allow me to quit Chinese studies and instead transfer to UST, a Catholic university, the following school year for my high school. I was overjoyed when Papa and Mama both agreed, although they never asked me why I slid to second place in English when I graduated from elementary that year. I was happy, though, to retain the first honor in my Chinese class that same year.

All of us except Bongga and Carol transferred to the University of Santo Tomas when we reached high school. Bongga finished his English and Chinese high school at St. Stephen's while Carol enrolled at Centro Escolar University. During high school, Eddie, my brother was my perennial headache. Every time he comes home with a note from the principal to bring his mom to school because of misbehavior, Mama would ask me to go in her stead. Much as I didn't want to, I really had no choice but face the principal. Oh, the price of being an older sister.

# Home For Lunch

"Hi! Ma! We're home!" we shouted as we entered the door. "What's for lunch?" all asked in unison. We have just come home from school. The *calesa* we rode in has left. We have only enough time to eat lunch and we would be going back to our afternoon classes immediately afterwards.

Mama is still in the kitchen finishing up her cooking. The sudden barking of her hungry brood has raised up her stress level. "Is it twelve o'clock already?" And as we peered into what was cooking, she would say good-naturedly, "Lunch will be ready soon. You kids! You should learn to wait. Even in restaurants, you need to wait a while for your food." Meanwhile, the maid has started setting the plates and silverware on the table. She brings in the cooked dishes one by one starting with the big platter of hot piping white rice. The soup dish comes in a big ceramic bowl. And the rest of the dishes follow, a vegetable dish, fried fish, and regularly another saucy dish like adobo.

Putting our bags down, we hurriedly take our seats and start eating. In about ten minutes or so, *A-Kuh* and *Sa-Kuh* (third Uncle Luming) together with the other employees from the store would be coming as well to take their lunch. Papa comes home much later around one o'clock after *A-kuh* goes back to the store to replace him. Yes, Mama cooks a lot for all of us every day.

We are fast eaters. We finish in ten or fifteen minutes max. Being part of a big brood makes this necessary. We were really not taught to eat fast. The habit just grows into you because you are aware that there are others waiting in line to eat. But this doesn't mean we discarded table manners because Mama has not been remiss in reminding us of manners while eating. We were taught not to lay our arms on the table because doing so is not only bad manners, but impinges on the space of the one seating beside you. We were trained to hold our spoon between the thumb and forefinger with the mid handle pressing on the middle finger. It was considered uncouth to grab the spoon with the four fingers with the thumb sticking out. It was considered bad manners to slurp and make a lot of noise while eating. Later on I would realize that these points were regarded differently in different cultures and even within the subcultures of one's country. In other regions in the Philippines, burping is a sign of appreciation for the food. Eating with our hands is A-okay and makes eating more enjoyable especially when out on a picnic or when dining on seafoods. Among older relatives, it was totally all right to use a toothpick after eating. And Papa always puts up his feet on his chair when eating especially at night. I guess there really is no absolutely right or wrong way when it comes to etiquette. All is dictated by the customs and tradition of the milieu where one grows up in.

Around twelve ten, *A-kuh* would arrive and with him the other store employees. *A-kuh* was always cheerful and looks forward to the food Mama cooks. He loved the soup dishes a lot. I remember one dish he really enjoyed was the fish ball soup. After he has finished his meal, he enjoyed tarrying at the kitchen where Ma is still cooking. *A-kuh* would occasionally get a fork and eat some more of the fish balls. I think Ma enjoyed seeing people liking and loving her food. Another favorite of *A-kuh* was the fish head soup with noodles. Mama fries the fish head first and later puts it in a soup. She adds cabbage slices and thick noodles to the broth. It was good. Although at that young age, I didn't actually like it that much.

One of our employees was a Bicolano man named Bonnie. Bicolanos come from the southern region of the Philippines and are known for their very hot foods. I used to be amazed when Bonnie eats *dinuguan*, a pig's blood stew cooked with minced pork and chili. For every spoonful of the viand, Bonnie would put one *siling labuyo*, the small chili peppers which are cruelly hot. Wow! I always thought to myself, "I wonder if his tongue ever gets burned." Tirong, on the other hand, never ate anything other than *bangus* (milkfish) with his rice. So, we grew up seeing Mama cook fried *bangus* every single day. I was amazed at how Mama never seemed to complain about this in spite of the extra trouble it gave her. Everyone knows how frying *bangus* is like waging a war with firecracker spurts from the hot oil and the consequences were all too evident on Mama's smooth skin. Holding the cover over the pan and expertly dodging the hits, Mama appears like a warrior engaged in a swordfight. In spite of the fact that she has gained a lot of expertise frying *bangus*, Mama has a lot of scars on her arms to show for this feat. Oftentimes, what seemed like moles on her arms were actually burns from the flying sizzles from the frying pan.

Eating at Mama's table is like reliving the multiplication of the loaves over and over again. Food was always served in serving platters on the table. We eat whatever we want and however much we want. The maid would refill the serving plates as often as needed. Food has never been rationed at our table and after each meal, everyone is full and satisfied. But there was always enough food for everyone. I suppose each one of us instinctively knew to leave some for the others who will still eat.

Luming, my mom's younger brother called *Sah-Ku* was a slow eater. He really takes his time eating. He looks a bit like Pat Boone. He was really handsome. He always took a shot of brandy with his meal because he had an enlarged heart and I guess takes this for medication. We loved Luming because after eating, he would often pull a stool in the kitchen, and we would gather around him while he tells us stories of a new movie he had watched. He often asked us in jest to pay him ten centavos each to hear his stories.

Unfortunately, Luming died at a very young age of twenty-nine. I remember that day. It was nearing noontime and Mama was cooking a Kapampangan dish "*burong dalag*". She actually buys the *buro* or fermented fish in the market and cooks it with garlic and tomatoes. Only Mama and I eat this dish. The others didn't like it because it tastes sour due to its fermented rice and fish. It was almost eleven o'clock when all of a sudden a cousin came shouting that Luming has died! *Sah-Ku* had been absent from work for almost a week already because of the flu. Apparently, he developed an allergy to his medication and succumbed to cardiac arrest. My aunts told us that he was even joking the night before because he had just eaten *singkamas* and remarked that he would proudly tell St. Peter in the next life about it. The internment and funeral procession for *Sah-Ku* was solemn and sorrowful. He was so young and was still a bachelor. So the music that was played during the procession was "Ave Maria", a sonorous and really sad song. And Tony, my cousin who happened to be his godchild, took the place of a son, carrying Luming's picture and bowing at the entrance of the cemetery. Tony's name was also inscribed in *Sah-Ku's* tomb as his son in keeping with the Chinese tradition that no man should enter the next life bereft of an offspring.

Anyway, after *A-kuh* goes back to the store, Papa would come home for lunch. For Papa, Ma always cooks a special dish. It would either be a small extra special noodle dish, or tempura shrimp, or steamed fish, or chicken soup with Chinese herbs. This shows just how special Papa is. I guess that is why some of my brothers liked to wait for Papa before eating. They knew it would always be extra good. Papa usually brings home a few pieces of cut and cleaned pineapple slices or watermelon for his dessert. He also always had a piece of banana afterwards.

Mama eats her lunch with Papa. By this time, she is usually so worn out from all the cooking that she is happy just to be able to finally sit down. I often noticed that she seldom eats a lot of the viands she had cooked. She would eat a lot of rice but was often content with just a piece of fish with her meal. All the aromas from her cooking must have been enough to fill her hunger.

Then after everyone has eaten, it is time for the house helps to take their meal. Mama doesn't scrimp in feeding her household, including the maids. In the evenings, Pa always had porridge instead of rice and uses chopsticks instead of fork and spoon. At times when there is much plain porridge left over from dinner, I noticed our maids liked putting sugar into it and eating it in place of rice.

# Study Time

It's almost six pm. The gathering dusk makes it hard for me to read my books in spite of the fully lighted dining room. All of us are home from school. We have had some snacks. I have taken a bath. And now, I am ready to tackle my homework. The rest of my brothers and sisters are also getting ready for study time. We get our respective seats around the long dining table. With a daily minimum of eight subjects, four for the morning English classes and four for the afternoon Chinese classes, we all needed to devote time to doing our daily homework. We didn't have the luxury of tutors, which a number of our classmates had. Some even employed our regular classroom teachers for their after school tutoring, all for a fee. Our parents didn't see the need for such extra expense. We were expected to attend our classes and to do our assignments. And we did not fail them. We were conscientious in our studies and we climbed the academic ladder year after year.

I get out my notebooks and proceed to tackle each subject. Once in a while, my younger brother Eddie would ask Bongga to help him with his math subjects. "Bongga, please explain this to me. I can't quite understand this equation." To which Bongga would reply, "Sure. No problem." After a while though, he would start getting irritated because he, too, was rushing with his own studies. Meanwhile, the light in our study area is starting to dim. The sun is setting and the dimming light is hard on the eyes. But we have gotten used to it. It was no surprise that all of us except Danny eventually needed to be fitted with prescription eyeglasses. Mama meanwhile was always around for moral support. At around seven o'clock she would go to the kitchen and cook up another dish or two for the evening meal.

I believe that good study habits are developed early on in a child's life. A good school and positive encouragement from the child's parents are integral to this formation. As far as I can remember, I have taken to school like a fish to water. I believe that not only I but all of my brothers and sisters enjoyed going to school. We even had a game we loved to play early in the morning on the way to school. While aboard a calesa and along a stretch of road on top of a bridge, we would beat each other in shouting "Shing Sheng Sheet Metal Works!" the name of a shop emblazoned on a poster at the left side of the road just as the calesa is descending from the bridge. The one who remembers to shout out the name first wins. The tongue twister and the game gives us an exciting start to an otherwise regular sleepy start of the schoolday.

We were more or less independent in the way we tackle our school assignments. I learned early on that resourcefulness is also a key to making school work both fun and easy. In elementary we had an assignment that required us to make an album of all the U.S. presidents. I got lucky when I went to the National Bookstore and chanced upon a comics magazine which precisely dealt on this topic. And it was so cheap I could afford to buy it. It came with pictures of all the presidents and with all the data I needed for the report. These little things usually gave me a sense of triumph and exhilaration.

High school required that that our parents sign our homeworks. This was one of the ways the teachers could be sure we really did it at home and not just copied it from our classmates. I remember my seatmate who was so good at signing her mother's name on her notebooks. I realized this was no guarantee after all but could also trigger some naughty and irresponsible behavior.

We were lucky that our parents provided the basic infrastructure that triggered good study habits among us. We were fed well and the home atmosphere provided the needed signal when it was time to study. Radio and television were off. And there was nothing else to do but settle down for homework.

Pa and Ma built the foundation for our responsible study habits. Almost all of us stood out academically. And all of us except Eddie managed to finish our college courses on time. Eddie was eventually able to graduate from college as well. This indeed is a crowning achievement for our parents. And we took all things in stride. It was a given that we would pass each school year and move on to the next level, each ending up with a college degree of his own choice. In hindsight, how I wish we had taken a family picture with our parents and all of us attired in our respective togas.

Like a majority of Chinese families, our parents required us not only to do well in our studies but to do our share in working at the family store as well. When the boys reached high school, classes were only for half a day every day. My father required them to work part time at the store for fifty pesos a month which he paid out of his own pocket. He figured that would keep the boys out of mischief. As for us girls, we did our share of cashiering when we reached college which required only a half day at school. Being working students did not prevent us from doing well in school.

Raising a big family is both a science and an art. Mama and Papa finally earned their degrees in living this out. They deserve the highest honors indeed.

# Household Helpers

"Masing! I don't have any polo shirt!" "Masing! Where are my white socks? I can't find them anywhere!" "Hey! Where is my notebook? I remember I left it here yesterday!" "My rubber shoes are so dirty. Quick, Masing! Give me a chalk so I can clean it." Normally, I would buy a sachet of "jobus" powder and mix it with water to properly clean my white rubber shoes. But during times like these when I simply had no time, I discovered it was faster to just get a piece of white chalk and rub it all over the shoes to give it a semblance of clean. These are just some of the chaos that greet our household in the mornings when everybody is hurrying to get ready. The logistics for our big family could be quite daunting especially on weekday mornings. At any given time, there are seven of the children still in elementary and high school. And we all needed to be up and out of the house by seven at the latest. That is why household helpers were a must in our family. Just washing and ironing all our uniforms and day clothes could easily take up the whole day.

I remember our maid, Masing, ironing up till ten o'clock most evenings. She typically starts ironing around four in the afternoon when Mama has finished cooking and the kitchen has been cleaned because she does her ironing in the kitchen. Masing would set up the ironing board near the kitchen table. Having taken down her day's wash from atop the small roof where she has hung the clothes to dry, she would fold them up one by one. Often she had a bowl of water nearby. Before folding the clothes she would sprinkle some water on them to soften them because usually the hot sun has dried them up too much. She would then fold them and arrange them neatly on a cardboard box. After doing the preparatory work, she would switch on the iron and proceed to do her ironing. On the window behind her, she would hang the newly ironed uniforms, pants, shirts, and dresses. I liked to talk to her while watching her iron clothes in the evenings when I didn't have anything better to do. I learned a variety of techniques in ironing from her which helped me a lot when I started my own family. She also enjoyed telling the stories of her childhood in Samar which she says has the biggest toilet in the world. She liked to shock me by telling me that while growing up in their province where toilets were commonly non-existent, they would go to the seashore which they regarded as their comfort room and do their business there. I remember going with her to Luneta on Sundays during her off days. She meets her friends who were mostly also domestic helpers here and they would just chat, eat, and while the afternoon away watching stage performances in the park.

House helps in the fifties and the sixties often stayed long in the families that they worked for. Usually they become part of the family they are serving and are treated as family too. Our early house helps stayed with us for ten, twenty years and like Masing continued to work for my sisters who have married and had children of their own.

Masing is now called Lola Masing by our own children. She has been with the family since we were very young. Only a few years older than my eldest sister, she has grown up and gotten old along with all of us. She was originally from Samar, a province in southwest Philippines. And she was in her teens when she came to work for our family. There was a time when she left us to work for other families. But eventually, she came back to work for Carol and then Linda when they got married and had children of their own. I sometimes chuckle to think that more than myself, she has managed to attend all the significant events in our respective families like the weddings of nieces and nephews, as well as the baptismal and birthday celebrations of the children who are now our grandchildren.

My mother treated our domestic helps well. They were paid on time and were allowed to go on off days once a week. And as always, Mama was never stingy when it came to feeding them. They were allowed to eat what was generally served on the table like everybody else. Although Mama never spared them from a tongue lashing when needed. Some of them like Carmen, a short, young and fairly cheerful girl from Bicol region just laugh off her reprimands. They knew that Aling Sion's bark was sharper than her bite. I can still remember Carmen giggling nervously when Mama is mad. She knows it will pass soon enough. We were more worried whenever Mama was unusually quiet, because that means she was not feeling well.

Ellen was another househelp whom I remember well. She is as short as Carmen and they were both with us at the same time. Both of them were from Bicol, a province in the Philippines known for its dishes cooked almost always with coconut milk and lots of chili peppers. Whereas Carmen is scatterbrained, Ellen is intelligent and very neat. They complemented each other. When the maids are happy, the family tends to be benefited because this means the maids could be expected to stay long. It was always a hassle when they leave. Then the process of asking around for referrals and searching for trustworthy and dependable househelp begins all over again and this is often not an easy task. And in the meantime, we have to divvy up the tasks among ourselves. Washing dishes would mean either Linda or myself for lunch or for dinner. Since I am the more obsessive one, I would often opt to do the lunch dishes. And that means, Linda will do the evening dishes. Linda likes to take her time being the type B person that she is. Oftentimes, the dishes would be stacked at the kitchen sink, and I would be at my wits end looking for Linda because it is her turn to do the dishes. I almost always find her talking leisurely with Papa. She couldn't be hurried. There were times I couldn't bear to see the pile of dishes to be washed and grudgingly start doing it while shouting at

Linda to hurry up and get to work. The easy go lucky one and the one who is always in a hurry to finish up. Guess who ends up on the losing end?

There was an Ilocana maid who worked for us as a laundrywoman. I remember her because she never wanted to eat anything else with her rice, except *muzcovado* sugar which is hard and dried. It is shaped like a coconut shell and she would grate it to break it down into little bits which she then eats with her rice.

We always had two maids at a time, one to clean the house and wash dishes and another one to do the laundry and ironing. Without being aware of it, Mama was excellent in her science of time and motion when she first decided that two maids at the least were needed for our big family. Imagine the loads of laundry we came up with especially with all of us going to school. A daily change of school uniforms was a must in Manila where it is constantly stiflingly hot and humid. Mornings were spent doing the laundry. Washing machines were unheard of and our laundrywoman washes the clothes in the open area behind the kitchen. Using both hands and in particular the knuckles to rub the clothes with detergent bar soaps especially along the collar where grime concentrates, the maid would sit on a low stool with a big round basin and several smaller ones around. Our school shirts are given a final rinse with cornstarch to provide a stiff starchy finish. Then she goes up the ladder to the roof where lines are strung for the clothes to dry under the sun.

The other maid is tasked exclusively with washing the dishes, cleaning the house, and accompanying Mama to the market. This involves waxing the floor and scrubbing it twice a day. Even the floors of the kitchen are given the same kind of work. In spite of the heavy workload, the maids are given sufficient time to rest during the afternoon and are allowed a day off during weekends. Many of them actually enjoyed working for us and becoming part of our family.

Domestic helpers have always been an indispensable part of most Filipino households. During the fifties and sixties, it was still relatively easy to hire competent and hardworking maids. In our family, since Mama was giving birth almost every year, it was an utmost necessity that we had someone who could be trusted enough to take care of the children while Mama was away in the hospital. Fortunately, at that time, many Filipinas who entered my mother's employ as helpers were industrious and trustworthy. Most of them were driven by poverty to seek this kind of work. Mama relied on friends and oftentimes our store hands for referrals. This was why we had a number of them who were province mates of Tirong from the Ilocos. We valued them a lot because they tended to stay long, were hardworking, and most resigned only when they were already about to get married. Nowadays, however, it is a rarity to get such good house helps. With the opening of overseas markets for domestic workers, they are fast becoming a vanishing breed for the local market. Many of them would rather try their luck abroad, and majority consider local employment a temporary stint at most.

# Home Cures for Simple Ailments

"Mama, my tummy aches!"

"Ma, I have a fever…."

"Ma, I think I am sick… I think I'm coming down with the flu."

"Ma, my tooth aches…waaah!"

These were familiar complaints in our house. With nine children living in a small two bedroom apartment, it was not unusual to find the children coming down with the flu one after the other. At times, seasonal afflictions like measles or mumps would strike one child and pretty soon, all the rest of the brood would follow. Fortunately, Mama was familiar with medicine, having worked at a pharmacy for the most part of her single adulthood. She became adept at treating our common illnesses by herself. During those times, one could easily buy medicines, including antibiotics, over the counter even without prescriptions. As long as you know what the usual medicines to take, you could be self-sufficient in regards to your health. So with her knowledge of common cures, Mama always took it upon herself to treat us whenever we got sick with the common flu, or measles, or diarrhea. Health and medicine were not a myth with her, and so this attitude was passed on to us, as well.

I still remember some of the common remedies then, like lomotil for diarrhea, paregoric for stomach aches (ugh! the taste of this liquid medicine is as bitter as it sounds), Benadryl for coughs, Saridon for headaches, A-P histallin for flu, Creamalin for stomach acidity, Chamomile lotion for skin itch in cases of measles or heat rashes, etc. There were times when the severity of the illness necessitated that we be seen by a doctor. During such times, the practice was for the doctor to prescribe a medicine. Prescriptions then were written which involved a mixture of different ingredients which the doctor wrote down and which the pharmacy formulates for the patient. If we developed a fever, we knew what would come up next. It was a trip upstairs to the bedroom with Mama and an enema bottle and potty. I didn't look forward to this but there was no way out. My mom believed that colon cleansing was the first and primary cure for more serious infections accompanied by fevers. Mumps was a childhood disease that children could not avoid and Ma would mix a concoction of a blue dye with vinegar. It smelled awful but we had no choice but to suffer it as she rubs it on our neck to alleviate the pain and the swelling.

I suffered from earaches often and I remember Ma bringing me to a popular EENT specialist named Dr. Ilano whose clinic was just a few blocks away from home. This was the same doctor who treated my cataract when I was barely four years old. My right eye had turned white for no apparent reason than that the maid had allowed me to go to sleep with my wet hair. Ma panicked when she saw my pupil turning white. What I remember next was her bringing me to Dr. Ilano and a heavy army blanket was used to tightly roll me in. A metal-like contraption was placed over my eye and the rest I no longer remembered. I guess he must have put me to sleep. When I woke up, Ma tried to ease the tension by telling me she was going to give me five centavos every time I allowed her to drop an eye medicine on my eye. Of course I gladly agreed. But I never did remember receiving the promised payment. Perhaps as a result of this eye problem, I remained severely nearsighted all my life.

We also had a family dentist. His name is Dr. Quiazon. His clinic was in Avenida and is located in a small side street. It was within walking distance for us. There is a small door leading to his clinic in the second floor of an old building. We had to go up a flight of stairs which was dimly illuminated. Climbing this flight of stairs always gives me the creeps. Going to the dentist is one of those must experiences which I have always dreaded. It starts when my tooth aches or when Ma detects a misalignment in a new permanent tooth. This always signals that it is time to go to the dentist. With my chest pounding, I go with Ma to the clinic. We climb up the narrow flight of stairs. Even going up the stairs feels icky. On top of the stairs, we come upon a swinging window which is yellowed from age. It has the

name of Dr. Quiazon, DD. Upon entering, I immediately
see the dental chair with all its contraptions. There are two
chairs in the corner for the companions to sit. Actually, Dr.
Quiazon is a kind, middle aged man. He has glasses and he
always seems happy to see us. I know he doesn't charge
much. I remember once when Linda and I went there. I
decided to go first. The dentist had me open my mouth. I
remember crying so loud. I was so afraid. Then I felt the
needle pierce through my gum. The anesthesia was injected
in front and back of the targeted tooth. After a few minutes
of waiting time, the numbness began to set in. By this time,
my wail had simmered down. All I could feel was my lips
feeling numb and I imagined it must have looked swollen
from the feel of it. Then, using his metal pliers, I felt the
dentist clamp the tooth, and with a strong, determined pull,
the tooth came out!!! It was over. Dr. Quiazon quickly got
a thick wad of cotton ball and pushed it down on the
bleeding cavity. It's finished! I was smiling now. And I
happily nudged Linda, "Hey! It's okay! It didn't hurt all that
bad." It's Linda's turn now. And she doesn't know whether
to cry or to believe me.

Another well remembered resource of Mama whenever
we had fever was to bring us to the fireman at the nearby
fire station near Sta. Cruz Church. Why a fire station?
Because the "*hilot*" or chiropractor we were going to see
was a fireman. He had natural healing power. By
manipulating our muscles and joints, he takes out the
blockage which he believes is causing the infection. There
is no pain involved. He uses a little oil to ease the kneading
of the flesh. And he does it all for free. Many parents resort

to this natural cure. And at times, the line could be long. Some say it's superstition but I could swear there is a science to it and, of course, faith in the healer. Surprisingly, our modern civilization is going back to this practice. It is truly medicine at its basic essence, "first do no harm". Ma had great faith in the fireman/healer, principally because he charges no fees for his service. Ma believes that these skills are God given, and once the healer starts using it for a fee, she believes his power disappears. Mama, however, always gave him a donation afterwards.

Ouch! It took an instant before my mind registered that I have cut my finger while chopping a piece of onion. I panicked at the bright red blood fast oozing out from the cut. And then the sharp pain started. Waah!! Pain and fear came out of my mouth. Mama quickly took me to the sink and washed the finger, all the while saying "Don't worry. *Malayo sa bituka iyan."* meaning "there is nothing to be afraid of. It is very far from your gut." This was my mom's favorite statement whenever we get scared of any ailment. As a child, I figured that so long as a wound or a gash is far from your innards, there is really no need to fear. My mom's mantra stuck well.

Another practice is whenever one of us accidentally swallows a fishbone and it gets lodged in the throat. Mama would give the child a piece of banana and ask him to get a big enough bite of it and to immediately swallow it without chewing first. Sometimes the bone goes down with the banana. Sometimes it doesn't. In my case I would sometimes get too full swallowing so much banana. Often after repeated attempts to clear my throat, Mama would casually look at my hair and from out of nowhere she would bring out a piece of fishbone and say, "See…here it is. It has jumped out of your mouth" If I believed her, I would soon forget about the whole thing and true enough it wouldn't be there anymore. One solution we have for this predicament is to call Ernie, my cousin who lives in Trinidad. Ernie was born a breech baby and because of this it is believed that he has the power to remove stuck fishbones in people's throats. Ernie comes to the house, wets his finger with his saliva and uses this to massage the throat of the victim. And oftentimes it works. Magic or superstition? I never found out the answer.

Mama has a number of food allergies. She cannot eat oysters at all because this brings on an immediate onset of ulcer. Her natural remedy is to drink warm milk and eat some crackers. If it is really bad she takes in creamalin tablets. When old age brought on severe rheumatoid arthritis, Mama suffered greatly. She made a concoction of alcohol filled with very hot chili peppers. And Papa would massage this on her legs nightly. For her diabetes, Mama was put on a restricted diet by her doctor. She had to eat brown bread instead of rice. At times, she would toast the bread on the stove and when I tasted the toasted brown bread, I figured it wasn't bad at all.

Nowadays when I look at the assortment of over the counter panaceas for common ailments, I can see that Ma was actually right in many of her common sense remedies. She was, in this respect, ahead of her times.

# Uniquely Pinoy Snacks

*MAMA*!!! *PABILI*!!! No, I'm not calling my mom. I'm calling an ambulant vendor selling native rice cakes, and translated loosely, "Mister!!! Please come over, I want to buy". Afternoons at home during vacation time are enjoyable because of numerous ambulant vendors plying the neighborhood streets with their varied snack fares. A favorite for us children with our limited monies is the *magpuputo* (rice cakes vendor), the old man with his *puto* and *kutsinta* contained in two huge aluminum covered pans which he hangs on his shoulders with a long wooden pole. He is barefoot with skin charred by the punishing heat of the daily sun. We are always amused by his antics because once he comes over we would ask him what he is selling. He would say *puto*, *kutsinta*. And as he utters these words, he would touch the aluminum cover and would quickly withdraw his hand as if he got burned. Then, he would remark in a singsong voice, "*Bagong luto at mainit-init pa*" (meaning it's freshly cooked and still hot). Of course we would burst out laughing because everyone knows his wares are cold as stone, although truly yummy. And with a sprinkle of grated coconut, we part ways with our few centavos.

The *magtataho* (soy drink vendor) is an all-time favorite even today. He also carries his wares on a wooden pole over his shoulders where a circular stainless steel container sits filled with three compartments, a big one holding the soft silken tofu and two smaller compartments holding the caramelized sauce and the pearly white tapiocas. Oftentimes, we forego his little plastic cups and bring our own bigger bowls to be filled up. Children crowd around him, waiting for their turn to be served. This vendor comes every single afternoon like clockwork and has successfully blended with the colorful mosaic of Filipino neighborhoods.

During summer days, another familiar sight in the streets are the little pushcarts driven by ambulant peddlers selling different kinds of seasonal fruits like green mangoes, yellow ripe mangoes, pineapples, young coconuts, bananas, *santol* (which is uniquely Filipino), and *tubo* or sugar cane rods. The man selling green mangoes and equally sour *santol* which are round fruits with a thick yellow peel displays artistic techniques of peeling the fruits which adds to the color of his trade. Taking a mango by one hand, he holds a small paring knife with the other hand and proceeds to cut the peel in slices. He makes equal lengths and widths of these slices and as he finishes, he removes the peel now looking like the shapely petals of a flower. He does the same with the *santol*, only this time, he makes horizontal cuts instead of vertical cuts. And once again, he ends up with the peel perfectly shaped like petals. A scoop of *bagoong* comes with our mangoes and for the *santol* simple rock salt.

Sugar cane is peddled in a rundown wood cart and usually, the peddler is in sleeveless t shirt and short pants. His single tool is a long *bolo* (knife). The cane sticks are arranged in various sizes and prized accordingly. I usually choose the thinner ones because they tend to be softer. Once I make a choice, the vendor proceeds to cut the thick violet skin in long firm strokes of his *bolo*. He leaves a portion of the skin at the end which serves as the handle. One needs a good set of teeth to bite off the flesh of the sugar cane, chew and suck the sweet juice out of it and then throw out the pulp. The procedure can easily overwhelm a lot of people's teeth. Surprisingly though I used to see old folks with missing front teeth biting at these rods with abandon.

The dirty ice cream vendor appears during various times of the day. I don't know why the term dirty ice cream when we children loved the taste of this poor man's ice cream which comes in simple flavors of cheese, mango, *ube*, and chocolate which is a weak version of real chocolate. The cart the vendor uses has two small wheels and two wooden handles which he uses to push the cart. But its body is painted with colorful bold designs much like the *jeepneys* and reveals once again a seemingly basic artistic bent of the common Filipino. We buy one or two scoops of ice cream often combining the flavors and asking that it be put in sugar cones. The vendor obliges us with a small thin tissue which he wraps around the cone. We could also ask that it be placed instead on soft round bread. We always knew when the ice cream vendor is around because we hear his bell which announces his presence.

Being a tropical country, the Philippines abounds in coconut trees. Increasingly the healthful benefits of coconut juice as a natural and tasty diuretic is being discovered by many. I believe that the coconut tree is one of the truly precious wealth of the country. Dubbed as the tree of life, all parts of this wonderful tree have seen practical usage from its shiny smooth leaves to its fruits down to its roots. In the streets of Metro Manila, the ubiquitous *buko* (young coconut) is both a source of livelihood for many poor Filipinos and a refreshing natural health drink. Starting from early morning, the wooden cart holding a full cache of young coconuts can already be seen starting its day at our neighborhood. The sunburned man takes his usual post at the corner of Mabolo. His main tool is the sharp *bolo* which he uses to first remove the husk of the coconut after which he proceeds to chop off the top hard wooden shell to reveal the gleaming white coconut meat underneath. He then pours the coconut water onto the container of the buyer and with the use of a flexible knife like gadget, he scrapes the meat off and pours it onto the same container. What we get is a refreshing drink of *buko* juice with delectable bits of soft sweet *buko meat*. Truly worth every centavo one pays for.

*Baluuuuuuuut! Baluuuuuut!* goes another tempting street food as we settle in for the night. This hard boiled treat of

very young duck, fetuses really, is something one finds hard
to resist in the times that one has a little money left over
from the day. It is more expensive than our daytime treats
and only once in a long while do we indulge in *balut*. In the
sixties, it probably costs around forty centavos a piece
which was quite expensive for us teen agers. The round
basket housing these goodies has a blanket covering the
warm eggs which never seem to lose their warmth. It is
almost reverential how these chicks which never get to be
born are at least cradled in warmth and comfort as they are
peddled in the late evenings all over the streets of metro
Manila. The *balut* vendor hands us a pinch of salt neatly
wrapped in a tiny white bond paper and as we crack open
the *balut*, our lips are quick to catch the savory fluid that
oozes out. The whitish yellow yoke appears, then the tiny
head followed by the black downy feathers and one cannot
help but marvel at how truly juicy and delicious it is. And
the price is always worth it. The perennial partners of the
*balut* are the packets of crispy *chicharon* which with a vinegar
dip seal the night. With the tummy full once again, we
happily decide to finally call it a day.

# The Games We Play

During the fifties and sixties, games children play were often dictated by the things they have on hand. There were no such things as ready-made high tech toys and gadgets like today. Often, we made do with bits and pieces of bottle caps or popsicle sticks. Our parents could not afford to buy the dolls and toy cars which could be found sparingly in department stores. I personally don't remember having my own doll. We had to be creative and on hindsight, it was more fun and challenging this way.

Once in a while, Mama would bring home miniature clay pots and pans from the market. We enjoyed these because we were able to cook real rice in them. Using crumpled paper and charcoal, we would actually cook rice. Of course, we did it in the kitchen where Mama could supervise us. And it was always a delight to finish cooking, because the aroma from rice cooked in clay pot was way better compared to rice cooked in aluminum pots. I guess, having lived in the city all our lives, we were not aware that this was common stuff in the province where cooking in clay pots and using charcoal to cook was the practice.

There were also times when Mama would buy insects like beetles from the market. We would tie up these insects using thin strings and let them fly around like kites. Again, insects were a source of much curiousity for us city bred kids. We didn't see much of them in the cities except for pesky mosquitoes, cockroaches, and flies, which was probably why, we were clearly fascinated to get acquainted with species which were thankfully not considered pests. To actually see them up close and to play with them was something of a novelty and fun to say the least. Sometimes my brothers would put them in matchboxes and pit them against each other.

In the evenings with Ma and Pa off for late night movies in downtown Avenida, we girls would go down to the living room, rearrange the furniture and play house. We would fashion it in such a way that we have make believe living room, kitchen and dining room. Then, using the usual soft drink caps and popsicle sticks, we would have our own tea sets. We would play until the time Ma and Pa came home which was usually around midnight. Sometimes with Mama and Papa away at the movies, Masing would try and put us to sleep under the mosquito net in our bedroom. More often than not, she would fall asleep faster than us and sometimes she would still be asleep when we could already hear Papa knocking at the door downstairs. Seeing that Masing is still snoring, we would shout "Fire!! Fire!!" And she would wake up panicking "Where? Where is the fire?" And we would laugh and laugh! Another joke played on poor Masing.

Another mischief I remember playing was when I was helping mom fix her vinegar with chili. *Siling labuyo* or hot chilis in the Philippines were real small, and very colorful. They come in bright red, yellow, green, orange. I would be tasked with washing them and putting them in recycled vinegar bottles. Mama would then pour in vinegar so that it could soak up the hotness of the chili peppers inside. This was a common condiment especially with fried fish. While doing this one day, I saw my little cousin Archie at our door. I decided to give him a red chili. Thinking it was candy, he put it in his mouth, and sure enough, he let out a big howl! Then he quickly scampered away. That was real naughty of me. I can't remember if my aunt Ebeng scolded me for that or not.

During summer when it was too hot to stay inside the house, we would usually bring our improvised tea sets outside and play on the sidewalk. There were also a number of street games we liked to play aside from hide and seek. One game involved skipping. To play this, we would first draw lines on the sidewalk. Using a white chalk, we would draw rectangles which would be enclosed in a bigger rectangle. Then using our slippers as dice, we would hop over the unfilled rectangle. The player would advance through all the holes until she steps on the line, after which her time is up and the next player would have her turn. This game is called "Step/No".

Another game which we used to play was called *tumbang preso* in tagalog or translated loosely, "shoot down the can".

We put an empty evaporated milk can around four feet in front. The players then take turns hitting it with their slippers. If one is unable to hit the can, he would run to the space beyond the can to retrieve his slipper. The one guarding the can whom we call *taya* will try his best to tag the player who is retrieving his slipper and if he succeeds in tagging the latter, then he is freed from being the *taya*. The tagged player then becomes the next *taya*.

*Sipa* was another uniquely Filipino game. This involved either a small paper balloon or a fist sized iron disc with mop like strands which the player hits with the inner side of one foot. He needs to successfully hit it without it dropping on the ground. The more hits he makes, the higher his score. Sometimes we would buy a folded paper balloon. This gadget costs just a few centavos, and lasts quite a while, and is easier on the foot too.

All of us played *yoyo* at one time or another. This gadget involves numerous techniques in swinging the string and causing the *yoyo* to create amazing loops and swirls. The more skilled ones always loved to show off their skills on the streets to the awe and amazement of their playmates. Soft drink companies regularly came out with promos using *yoyo* as giveaways. Hula hoop was another favorite game especially among the girls . Aside from the thrill of winning, we enjoyed this game a lot as it always succeeds in releasing our tremendous energies as children .

For a few centavos we could buy a small tube of plastic balloon from the corner store. We had real fun blowing the balloons. The boys loved to play *teks*, a card game. They would buy play cards from the *sari-sari* store, sit down on the pavement, and play. They always seemed so serious and intent while playing *teks*. I never did learn the mechanics of their game but I would see them walking proudly around with the cards held tightly in their hands. Usually the boys played with boys and the girls with girls. I guess there was an instinctive segregation among the little kids of the neighborhood. But we considered everyone our friends.

Jump rope was another game the girls enjoy playing. The boys, on the other hand, sometimes play basketball right on the street. They usually put the basket at the street corner where it was safer for the players. Oftentimes my brothers would rent bicycles from another street and ride it around the neighborhood.

One of Bongga's classmates was a badminton champion of the Philippines. He often came to the house. Once we begged him to teach us badminton. He gamely agreed. And guess where we played? Out on the street right outside our house. We had to stop every so often though whenever a car passes. But learned badminton we did .

Street games fostered much camaraderie and social interaction. It didn't cost much and it fostered sportsmanship and creativity. It also provided us with lots of sunshine and exercise .

# Television At Last

Television was a luxury which we didn't have until much later. As little kids, we used to go to a neighbor's house to watch the noontime show Student Canteen. This Chinese family was the first to own a television set in our neighborhood. It wasn't surprising because they owned a business selling Sony appliances. And they didn't mind us children going over to their living room to watch tv. Student Canteen was so popular that students going home for lunch couldn't wait to see it. Lunch was gobbled up so that one could catch up on the show.

I think I was around fourteen years old when Papa finally brought home a second hand tv set. It was encased in a wooden cabinet that could be closed. He bought it from a friend. This excited us no end because we would be able to finally watch television in our own house. For a while there was a lot of bickering among us as to what channel to watch. But since there were so few channels available anyway, these arguments on what programs to watch eventually died down.

I remember Mama's favorite show was the wrestling matches. It was typically shown at around six thirty in the evening. And during such days, our open door would quickly fill up with spectators. The TV set was placed in the living room facing the door. And it didn't take long before neighbors and passersby got wind of this exciting program. For a lot of people then, this was an exciting new sport. Filipinos are big fans of boxing, but this was something else. We particularly liked the match between midgets. They were so light and fast on their toes, and they didn't seem to get hurt as they get hurled and tackled. The dirty tricks of the players really sent emotions of the audience sky high.

It was especially funny to watch Mama during these wrestling matches. She always gets emotional and often enough would scream, shout, and scold the wrestlers, sounding a lot like a sports anchor. She really seemed to feel what the fighters were feeling. We often laughed at the sight of Mama getting so emotionally involved with watching wrestling. And with the crowd outside shouting and yelling as well, the half hour show would ignite so much enthusiasm and exhilaration that everybody felt exhausted but good afterwards. Mama didn't mind the crowd at the door. She figured it was good to share this new blessing that has come into our home.

Of course our favorite show then was Student Canteen with Eddie Ilarde, Bobby Ledesma, Pepe Pimentel, and Leila Benitez. Coming home from morning classes, we never failed to put on the tv to catch our favorite program. We particularly enjoyed its regular fare of singing and I.Q. contests. Early evening shows like the "Nida Nestor Show" and the "Sebya Mahal Ko" comedy series were runaway favorites. Of course "John and Marsha" in later years stayed at the top of our list for many years as well. TV sitcoms in the Philippines then were wholesome and really funny. A common thread that ran in these sitcoms was always that of a typical lower middle income Filipino family living a normal hand to mouth existence. But rather than focus on the problems and seriousness of life, it always manages to bring out the humour in the common misadventures of a household. No episode ever ends without eliciting loud bursts of laughter and enjoyment as the audience accompanies the characters in their daily exploits. Filipinos are a happy people in general and the comedy series in both radio and television in the sixties and the seventies are in part responsible for cultivating this enviable cultural trait. No matter how hard up a family is and no matter the gravity of many of the natural calamities that visit the country on a regular basis, this inherent capacity to see the okayness and humor of life enable its people to bounce back time and time again. This plus an innate religiosity, no matter how lacking in depth as some people see it, is an indispensable reason for the hardiness yet essential lightness of spirit that characterize a common Filipino. No wonder Filipinos are a happy people. They almost always manage to see humor in the everyday happenings of life.

Television then was in black and white, but no matter, it introduced a lot of fun and variety to our family life. It was much later when the daily evening news became part of Philippine television. In spite of the addition of television in our daily lives, we were disciplined enough to always put study and homework first before anything else. Our values regarding education were ingrained enough by this time, and we always knew it came prior to television. To this day, I can't help but be amazed at how well we have internalized our discipline in study, without our parents exerting undue pressure on us. I guess studying for us became increasingly effortless as it eventually became almost a habit.

# Lauriat Time

A lauriat is a symbol of celebration, camaraderie, community, family. It speaks of rejoicing, reunions, closeness, laughter, and children, kinship, food. My father had a penchant for celebrating every major occasion with a lauriat treat for the whole family.

Chinese Lauriat was derived from the Hokkien dialect, *lao-diat*, meaning celebration or fiesta. The banquet consists of round tables which seats from twelve to fourteen people. The tabletop is often a bright red tablecloth and at the center is a lazy susan where the dishes are served. The host or hostess stands at the entrance of the function room to greet the guests and then show them to their seats. While waiting for the feast to begin, the guests would nibble on the peanuts and melon seeds that are provided on the table. Hot tea served in tiny tea cups are also made available. When all the guests have arrived, the host would signal the head waiter that the feast can now begin. Lauriat time is always fun time. We get to eat celebratory foods which are not only pleasing to the palate but are also truly a feast for the eyes.

The banquet starts off with a big round plate of cold appetizers. Arranged in a colorful circle, we have portions of century eggs sliced in wedges, white chicken cut in bite sized portions, pig's brain presented in sweet sugary dices, crunchy strings of jellyfish, pork asado slices, fresh cucumber slices with marinated sweetened daikon radish and pickled carrot slices to cool the palate. Of course this is just the beginning. And the hungry guests dig in, eagerly anticipating the parade of mouth-watering dishes yet to come.

The plate of appetizers usually disappears in a flash. And seeing the plate emptied, the waiters promptly bring in the next dish. If the particular celebration is a birthday, birthday noodles are served immediately after the appetizers, and the birthday song is played throughout the banquet. Otherwise, what follows is bird's nest soup with little hardboiled quail eggs floating on top. The waiter artfully ladles the soup from the giant soup bowl into tiny bowls. When he is done, we eagerly reach out for our individual bowls. A hot creamy soup is good to down the sweet and sour appetizers that have just been savored.

Next in line is, yup, you guessed it right, pigeon halves fried to perfection and seasoned with salt and pepper, and awakened to full flavor by a pinch of squeezed lemon. This is a hands down favorite with everybody. Oftentimes the head of the pigeon is kept on. Crisp to the bone and yet lean on the meat, the portion is enough to not fill one up but whets the appetite for more. Of course, everyone gets only one piece each. And this portion is half a pigeon cut lengthwise. This dish is always accompanied by a bed of crunchy prawn crackers. All of us beat one another to get some of these crackers because they disappear fast. The children especially devour it.

The dish that follows is abalone with whole shitake mushrooms and tender bokchoy steeped in a sweet brown sauce. In the sixties, abalone was still affordable and the fresh, succulent, fleshy abalone served in a lauriat are cut in sizable portions, unlike these days when abalone is so pricey one only gets to have a few thin strips of it in a dish. The mushrooms that go with this dish are the huge whole ones which one usually gets only in Hongkong. It is full and juicy and simply melts in your mouth. The green slightly cooked bokchoy completes the triad.

After everyone has gotten his fill of the stewed saucy abalone and mushroom, the waiter removes the serving plate and comes in with another huge plate filled with fried golden prawns. These are skewered and sit amid a fruit salad lying on a bed of lettuce greens. The crunchy batter of the prawns goes well with the fruit salad smothered with rich creamy mayonnaise. This, too, is an easy favorite.

Following the fried dish is another saucy dish. this time, a stewed whole chicken with sticky rice filling. The brown sauce is rendered more flavorful by full, round Chinese mushrooms and roasted chestnuts. I have always loved this dish but have yet to cook it. This is a dish favored by the older Chinese.

By this time, the children in the different tables have gotten enough of eating and are starting to climb down their high chairs for a chance to stretch and run around. Meanwhile the adults have worked up enough steam to tackle the remaining dishes still waiting to be served. Steamed lapulapu in white sauce is served next. The fish used for this dish is huge, easily weighing two kilos. Only really fresh, live lapulapu is used and since it is steamed, the juice is preserved and enhanced by the white sauce. Simple and elegant, the steamed lapulapu is my Papa's favorite. As a host, my father is excellent, always ready to serve his guests and tackle the carving or the turning of the fish once one side of it has been consumed. But the fish head is always reserved for my father, as it symbolizes seniority and leadership. The freshness of the fish is evident in the taste and aroma of the dish. I have noticed the Chinese people's talent for serving seafoods sans their characteristic fishy smell. I have yet to taste a seafood dish in a Chinese restaurant that smells or tastes fishy. I suppose it is because they choose only the freshest produce and with ginger and sesame oil are always able to come up with a perfect dish.

A fitting finale to an evening of delicious eating is a huge platter of huge steamed male crabs. By the time the steamed crabs are served, a lot of the guests are already full. So the ones who have been waiting for the crab dish all evening and who were smart enough to leave room in their tummies for it, are more than happy to see that they have no more competition. They happily hunker down to taking their time with the dish. The steamed crabs are super fresh and yummy and their red color spells celebration all over.

They are served cracked and cut for easy handling by the guests. The guests freely use their hands to pick at the shells and suck out the meats. And with the kids out of the way, the adults are free to take their time with this refreshing dish. By this time, everyone feels full and the conversations and camaraderie continue.

If the noodles have not been served at the start of the feast, it is served as a final dish. Although by this time, everyone is truly full and the noodle dish is wrapped up together with the other leftovers and taken home by the host or the guests.

As a host, nothing satisfies my father more than seeing that his guests were truly satisfied and he had once again proven his skills as a host. Because it is the host who has spent the time to pick and choose the menu that would be served. Years of arranging for lauriat celebrations have honed my father's skill in choosing the best dishes and their combinations for a truly successful feast. My brother Eddie seems to have gotten this same knack and in our adult years would take over that function.

The table is cleared and in comes the dessert. As the waiters come in with the pinipig crunch, Magnolia's all-time favorite ice cream, the children scramble back to their seats. Yes, they know it is time for dessert. Usually, this is served with a bowl of fruit cocktail and lychees, and platters of sweet delicacies like sesame balls and mini cakes.

And so, another celebration comes to an end. Everyone is full. The conversations have been much enjoyed and the bonding complete for now. The family leaves with relationships deepened by food and camaraderie.

# Annual Excursions

It's six o'clock in the morning. Sunlight was fast streaming into our bedroom and I was still in dreamland. Then I heard Mama waking us up! "Come on you sleepyheads! Time to wake up! It's excursion day today!" My half asleep mind suddenly jolted awake!! Yes!! This is what we have been waiting for all week now. The day we go to Antipolo and Tagaytay! Yeheyyy!! Everybody was awake all at once.

Mama has been up since five o'clock. Together with the two maids, she has been very busy preparing the dishes we would be taking with us. Last night she has already finished cooking the chicken *adobo* and the fried chicken. This morning, she prepared an additional noodle dish and rice and the maids are now finishing the dozens of sandwiches we would be taking as well. Yummy!! Our excursions always meant food, food, fun, and more food.

Every year at around May, our family embarks on an excursion which includes all our cousins, aunts, and uncles, and all our household helpers. The month of May is almost always the hottest part of the year in the Philippines. But it is also the merriest. It is marked with fiestas in different parts of the country. One of the most popular is the feast of Our Lady of Good Voyage in Antipolo, which is our first stop today. The church there will be packed with Sunday worshippers and parking was expected to be a horrendous problem. But that wouldn't be our concern because for this occasion Papa has hired a commercial bus and this would be the driver's problem. My mother has nine brothers and sisters and several of them have their own families. This easily brings the total number of passengers from the entire clan to around fifty and only a bus would be big enough to transport all of us. Of course, each group would also be bringing their own foods for the picnic. There would always be fried chicken, noodles, rice, beef stew, fried fish, fruits, salads, sandwiches and cases and cases of soft drinks. That's what we liked about these family affairs. We were always assured of more than enough food.

Everybody is wide awake now. We hurry to gulp down our breakfast and hurriedly dress up, excited to wear newly purchased shirts and jeans for the special occasion. Soon enough the chartered Saulog transit bus arrived. We're the first stop. After which we will fetch our other relatives who mostly live in the same compound in Magdalena. By God's grace, we're all finished and ready to board the bus. Mama too has finished packing up the foods and stacking them in the bus. Our cousins from Trinidad street have also arrived and at long last, everybody is accounted for, the house is locked up, and we're on our way.

By the time we begin our trip to Antipolo, traffic has already built up. Alongside the line of cars and buses, hilly terrains covered with reddish, clearly very fertile soil were visible. But the children couldn't care less. We were so happy to see each other again. It's bonding time. Non-stop chatting and eating has begun. The heat of the sun has also caught up with us. When we finally reached Antipolo, a number of us were already busy looking for restrooms. We contented ourselves with the make shift toilets that have sprung up in this small sleepy town. Public restrooms consisted mainly of holes in the ground. I felt icky but had no choice but use it. Then we heard Mass. The church was overflowing with people, and the electric fans scattered around the ceilings helped but a little to alleviate the heat of the noonday sun. Most everyone was fanning themselves. The homily of the priest, as usual, centered on the financial needs of the parish for the upkeep of the shrine. After about an hour, the mass finally ended.

Now we had time to ogle at the many goodies for sale outside the church. There were *suman* wrapped in yellow native palm leaves and sticky brown coconut cakes wrapped in banana leaves. The festive atmosphere was adorned with a wide variety of native fruits like *siniguelas*, mangoes, mini bananas called *senyoritas* still strung in their trunks, pineapples, *duhat*, and much more. Here and there, we could see stalls selling *lechon* and *dinuguan*. Colorful native hats and fans and plastic toys greeted our eyes. Peddlers of balloons eagerly approach the crowds of little children coming out from the church. The adults took some time buying the fruits and foods on sale. And we all heaved a sigh of relief as we climbed back up our bus for the second and the more exciting phase of the trip. We were headed next to Tagaytay.

We reached Tagaytay after more than an hour. Tagaytay is in the highlands where the air is much cooler. The view is also spectacular for us who are perennial city dwellers. The Taal lake and the Taal volcano are the main attractions here, and of course the chance to get out of the stifling heat of Manila even for just a few hours is a much desired blessing. The only drawback here is the lack of potable water. That is why we always made sure to bring enough soft drinks and drinking water for everyone. Otherwise we needed to buy them. Once there, we scouted around for a place to settle in for the day. We chose a recreation ground with a big wooden gondola where we could all fit in. It was like a big open ballroom. Everybody helped bring down the food and other paraphernalia from the bus. Then we ate our lunch. In spite of the fact that we have been snacking throughout the trip, everybody was famished. The air must have something to do with it, and of course, the fact that we were all growing kids with tremendous appetites. In no time at all, everyone was busy eating.

After lunch, the adults mostly wanted to just laze around and rest. But the children were raring to go to the horseback riding range which was nearby. For a fee, one could have a horse for an hour. It was quite easy to maneuver the horse. The trainer taught us how to pull the rope to turn the horse right or left, how to just trot, and how to pull it to stop. This kept us busy for most of the afternoon. Then we headed off for some sightseeing. Meanwhile, the adults who preferred to stay under the shade of the gondola were either napping or playing cards or mahjong. A number of them were just lazing around talking. Clearly they were trying to savor as much as they could of the clean cool breeze of the mountain air. Here at least one could breathe free and soak in nature as yet untarnished by the onslaught of urbanization.

Soon enough, the children are coming back one by one. They're hungry again and thirsty. Soft drink bottles are opened, paper plates are filled up and pretty soon, everyone is snacking again. Whatever is left of lunch are soon a thing of the past. At around five o'clock, it was time to pack up. We climb back up the bus. Everyone has had a satisfying, tiring, fun-filled, and memorable day. "This time again next year!" the children shouted as the bus dropped off its passengers one family at a time.

Years later when we were all grown up and married, the practice of an annual excursion for the clan stopped. But every once in a while, Papa would spearhead an excursion just for our family and this time with all the grandchildren. We continued the practice of hearing Mass first at Antipolo before we head on to Los Banos. There our favorite place was the City of Springs Resort where heated swimming pools and barbecue facilities are provided. We would rent around two rooms and while the children swam in the outdoor swimming pools, Mama and Papa would soak in the covered heated swimming pool that was rented by the hour. This was especially therapeutic for Mama's arthritis because the water in the pool was sourced from the hot springs of Mount Makiling. With the barbecue grills scattered around the outdoor pools, we would spend the whole day just eating and swimming. And when we finally head home, Papa would decide to drop by KFC in Roxas Boulevard for our dinner. Eventually Pa grew tired of going on these excursions and he would say in jest that instead of tiring himself, "it's much better to just take a shower at home and take a nap in my air conditioned room".

# Todos Los Santos – All Saints' Day

One area of life wherein the Chinese and the Filipino traditions are beautifully blended is in the reverence we accord our dead. The richness of both traditions is an invaluable part of my heritage as a Filipino-Chinese. And the time of the year when we celebrate this occasion is *Todos Los Santos*, or All Saints Day. We observe this on the first of November every year.

Our family started with having just one relative interred in the Chinese cemetery, the remains of my mother's father. His tomb is made of an unpretentious black marble. Made of sturdy and stable foundation, it is housed in a simple white cemented four walls with cemented seats and an aluminum roof. It really is quite simple in contrast to the other mansion-like structures of the rich Chinese. Then when my third uncle and grandmother died, the family had another similar structure built on an adjoining lot.

All Saint's Day is a big event for us as well as for the rest of the populace in Manila. All day long, throngs of people walk by foot to go to the cemeteries, bringing flowers, candles, incense, and food. There is a festive air all throughout the day. Lining the streets on the way to the cemeteries are stalls and stalls of vendors selling flowers, candlesticks, incense, soft drinks, and snacks. Cars are prohibited in order to accommodate the thousands of people who literally make a pilgrimage to visit their deceased loved ones.

I remember that this is one of the rare days when our textile store is closed. *A-kuh* and his family go to the cemetery very early in the morning. Papa and our family go there after lunch. Our other uncles and aunts and their families also go there on different hours of the day. Papa brings huge red candles with dragon carvings and plenty of *siopao*, dumplings, Chinese rice cakes, and a huge basket of local fruits like mangoes, bananas, *lanzones*, and *pomelos*. He fixes a spot on the floor beside the door of the tomb where he lays an offering of food for the gods. On the top shelf where the picture of the dead is placed, another set of fruits are auspiciously placed. Flowers are draped over the picture as well. Everybody brings in their own food including cooked rice and viands to last the entire day. And of course, it would not be complete without the children who look forward to the day as another outing celebration. As we arrive, we would each take two sticks of incense, walk to the center of my grandpa's tomb, bow our heads with the incense sticks clasped in our hands at the center of our chest. After we finish, we would stick the incense to the clay jar at the floor.

Once more, the cousins get a chance to meet up and touch base. We start the day by reciting the rosary. Linda and I used to bring a song booklet which we call song hits. We both might not sing well but we love to sing all the same, and songs from Sandra Dee, the Bee Gees, Andy Williams top the list. Then Papa would order cases of softdrinks for everyone. November is the season for *lanzones,* a fruit unique to the Philippines which are small cream colored round fruits with a thin skin which when peeled would show white juicy wedges of flesh with small seeds which could be very sweet. We consume kilos of it. The only downside is the sticky sap it leaves on your fingers as you peel it. Nevertheless, we really enjoy ourselves. Throughout the day, friends and relatives of the family come to give their respects and candles. There are so many candles lighted on each of the tomb that at the end of day, the melted wax is scooped up and gathered by the children and even relatives who would eventually process them into floor wax for the house.

Almost all the tombs have been painted white for this big day. Colored buntings are placed on top of the tombs held down by little pebbles as a sign that someone had already visited. The picture of the deceased is usually made a part of the tomb and his or her name inscribed on the front lower part. People coming in and going out of the cemetery is never ending, giving out a really festive atmosphere. I am sure the dead are very happy during this special day of the year reserved only for them. It is also the time for reunions for families who seldom get to meet during the year.

At about four o'clock in the afternoon, Papa would announce that it is time to go home. The awnings are removed by the men, the foods are packed up, and the place spruced up a bit. Then we begin the long trek out. It doesn't seem like an ordeal because one is part of thousands walking. Then as we reach farther out of the cemetery, we are finally able to get public transport for home.

# Duck Soup

The Thursday following All Saints' Day is duck soup day for the family. After remembering the dead, we, the living are reminded to partake of specially nourishing food for ourselves and that means special duck soup cooked with lots of Chinese herbs and spices.

Prior to this day, Mama would have bought at least one live duck. As with chickens, Mama has to slaughter the duck herself. Before she actually kills the duck, she force feeds it with a tablespoon of white vinegar. This will make it easier for her to pluck the duck's feathers. Unlike chicken feathers, duck down is more stubborn and take longer to remove. An hour after the vinegar feed, she is ready to start the process. She first prepares her bowl of raw vermicelli and her super sharp cleaver. Picking up the squealing duck, she tucks it under her arm with her hand tightly clutching the duck's beak and the maid firmly grasping the legs. With her other hand holding the cleaver, Mama then slits its throat. The bright red blood comes gushing out of the slit throat and drops straight down unto the bowl. Mama continues her tight grip of the duck until the poor bird stops quivering and Mama makes sure that the blood has been emptied. It is important that all the blood has been shed so that none of it clings to the meat when it is finally cooked.

The dead duck is then placed on a basin and boiling water is poured over it before Mama starts plucking the feather. Oftentimes, Ma has to use a tweezers to pull out the stubborn down remaining on the skin of the duck. This usually takes a little time. Then she cuts off the head, chops off the two wings, and proceeds to cut through the sides of the breast, removing the intestines, the gunk, and the innards. She cuts off the oily skin over the tail as well as the fatty piece underneath it. Then she chops off the duck into smaller pieces careful to cut through the cartilage, in order not to break the hard bones. She sets aside the heart, gizzards, and the liver. After this, she cleans up the cut duck in running water, rubbing salt first and removing the slime in between the skin and the lean meat. After this, she proceeds to prepare the other ingredients.

One key ingredient which goes into the duck soup is pork intestine. We call it "*ti-to*". Ma goes through a tedious process of cleaning and preparing pork intestine. She washes it with salt and vinegar and then boils it in vinegar again, after which it goes through another boiling process this time with water until Mama is satisfied that it is clean enough to include in the duck soup. She also has pork chops, beef tendons and sea cucumber as well as rectangular tofu slices which she has previously deep fried.

Mama sautés ginger slices allowing its aromatic sweet smell to be released before adding in the water for the broth. Then she puts in the duck together with the gizzards and the blood which by now has coagulated in its bed of vermicelli. She then adds in the pork chop, pork intestines, beef tendons and whole Chinese mushrooms, and of course, soy sauce and the handful of Chinese herbs and spices called "*si-but*". The pot is left to simmer for an hour or so until the meat becomes tender. Towards the end of the cooking process, sea cucumber, fried tofu, the liver and the heart are added to the pot. Oftentimes, Mama would scoop a small quantity of the broth, put it in a small casserole and add in "*koh-le*", another herb known to give strength and energy, and simmers this for another half hour. This extra nourishing concoction is, of course, for Papa.

Mama reserves the duck head for Papa as well. He likes the skin and meat in the cheeks and the eyes after which he cracks the skull to scoop the duck brain which is especially flavorful. Papa knows how much I like the duck head and shares some of it with me. Later on, Mama made it a practice to cook two ducks at a time so that Papa and I can have one head each. Mama finishes cooking the duck soup by early afternoon and the family has a truly nourishing dinner afterwards.

The family takes the duck soup for dinner. On this day, Papa takes bread with his duck soup instead of porridge which is his standard fare for supper. The rest of us eat our duck soup with rice. The work that goes with its preparation and the various ingredients and herbs make this a truly invigorating dish. Thus, we end another season of remembering the dead by nourishing the living.

# More Gastronomic Delights

The saying that "food is medicine" was given life in how Mama cared for Papa by coming up with dishes that were not only delicious but were intrinsically healing and nourishing at the same time. Aside from giving Papa soft boiled eggs and fresh carabao's milk for breakfast every single morning, she also regularly came up with food that had health and medicinal values.

Periodically, she prepared bird's nest broth which is known to sharpen one's vision. I remember having to remove the tiny hairs from clumps of dried bird's nest immersed in a bowl of warm water. This wasn't the easiest task because it required a concentrated effort to pluck out the tiny hairs in order to come up with clear and clean bird's nest which Mama would boil in water and chunks of sugar crystals. Once finished, the broth is sweet, refreshing, and cooling. Believing that it improves my vision, I would gladly accept a small bowl that Papa often shares with me.

Many afternoons, Mama steams ground beef saving the pure beef broth that is harvested from an hour or more of extraction. For this, she buys a kilo of fresh beef which she chops into a coarse grind. Then she gets two large bowls. One is set upright in the center of a big casserole filled with water. On top of this bowl is a smaller sized bowl placed upside down. Then around the side of the top bowl is placed the chopped beef. A piece of ginger is placed alongside the beef. The pot is then steamed for an hour or so. What results from this is a precious quantity of pure beef broth which ends up pooled on the bottom bowl. This extraction is given to Papa for his afternoon drink. And the cooked ground beef that is left behind is then transformed into a variety of equally tasty dishes. It was often turned into hamburger patties or meat balls. At times, Mama uses it as sauce for spaghetti. Or she would just sauté it with garlic, onions, and tomatoes and ketchup. For a while we relished the ingenious dishes that came from the left over ground beef. Eventually, however, the novelty of it wore off. And increasingly the children tired of these once eagerly awaited treats.

Almost every afternoon without fail, the maid would prepare a tall glass of *calamansi* juice for Papa which he takes upon waking up from his nap. Once in a while, Mama would have pig kidneys which she slices in a special way by first making crisscross cuts before cutting into bite size pieces. This she cooks with pork slices and the result is delicious soup filled with *misua* (vermicelli).

Chinese herbs and spices regularly find their way into Ma's chicken soup. Aromatic herbs with strange sounding

163

names like "*koh-lê*" "*tong-kuey*" "*sih-buf*" often in small pouches render the soup with specific healing properties and judging from the exotic, soothing aromas they exude, it must be true that they are possessed of magical tonic powers.

One practice which I didn't understand enough was how Chinese medicine bought from Chinatown undergoes a boiling process in a clay pot which ceases only when the liquid has diminished into the size of a small cup. It was ironic that Danny who was a doctor himself could not tolerate western medicines like antibiotics. My parents time and again observed that oftentimes when Danny was given antibiotics, he would turn listless and light headed which was clearly a sign of intolerance. Because of this, Papa oftentimes brought him instead to the Chinese drug store in Chinatown where a doctor would pulse him and prescribe some herbs and folk medicine. And true enough, it always managed to cure Danny of whatever ailed him.

When the children are down with the flu, it was usual for Mama to boil thin, yellow palm stems bought in Chinatown to come up with "*ham chao kuanh*"'a cooling drink that aids in faster healing. This is similar to sugar cane juice which is also commonly available in Chinatown.

We grew up essentially with the belief that one can stay healthy first and foremost by taking in nutritious and healthful foods. For Ma and Pa, food is the way to good health. A fusion of Chinese and Filipino dishes, as well as a combination of western and traditional Chinese medicine played an intrinsic part in our daily lives and with it the empowerment that comes with knowing that our health is, indeed, in our hands.

# On To High School

I enjoyed learning and going to school. High school was particularly memorable and enjoyable. Whereas elementary honed my reading, writing, and arithmetic, and proved to me that good work was always rewarded, high school showed me that camaraderie and peer socializing were fun. And not only that, but these years gave me the opportunity to put to work my organizational and leadership skills. This period in my life did a good job of providing a venue where these skills could be unleashed and developed. Needless to say, my parents were delighted that having graduated as an honor student from elementary entitled me to a full scholarship in the four years of high school.

I was fortunate to have been given the chance to engage in and lead a number of organizations like the editorship of our Graduation Yearbook, the Veritas. Being partly Chinese, I was also chosen to head the Chinese Student Association (CSA) as its female president. My writing skills were put to use by being the literary editor of the Aquinian, our school newsletter. These extra-curricular activities made my high school experience rich, interesting, colorful, and very much fun.

USTHS also demanded that we read a lot by requiring book reports every so often during our entire four years of study. I became a voracious reader, devouring such classics as Jane Eyre, Wuthering Heights, Pride and Prejudice, Sense and Sensibility, as well as the mystery series of Nancy Drew, Dana Girls, and Hardy Boys. Adulthood in later years saw me engaged in the genres of sagas, holocaust stories, Robin Cook novels, alternative medicine, inspirational books, and authors Neal Walsch, Bernie Siegel, Deepak Chopra, Andrew Weil, Ken Wilber, Eckhart Tolle, Rasha, etc. Reading widened my horizons and satisfied my hunger for seeking out the essence and meaning of life in its various forms. School opened up that world and this interest continues up to this day.

In high school, girl sessions were held in the morning and boy sessions in the afternoon. We were ranked according to sections depending on our academic standings. Being in section A had its perks. Not only did it carry prestige but it also provided a lot of fun especially during those occasions when out of fun we would come up with spontaneous presentations where we got to witness various talents of our classmates. I especially remember those who had exceptional singing and acting talents and those who could deliver oratorical and declamation pieces extra well. We got to stage these on the spur of the moment when teachers were absent. Fourth year was especially memorable because we were at the helm of all the extra- curricular organizations in school. That was also the first time when most of us got to know our counterparts in the boys section. Soirees and parties punctuated the final months leading to our graduation. We got scolded by our adviser when she found out we have met with the section A boys in informal gatherings. We reasoned out that we had to do this so that we could enjoy our graduation ball which would be an extravagant affair. Getting to know them ahead of time would succeed in breaking the ice before the much anticipated party. And sure enough, the graduation ball was a success.

I remember a poignant experience in the Chinese Students Association. We decided that for our part in a school wide presentation, we would present a traditional Chinese Engagement Ceremony. This is an elaborate ceremony where the groom and his parents go to the house of the bride-to-be bringing with them the required ceremonial Chinese baskets filled with delicacies, jewelry, and exquisite clothing materials as gifts. On hand to meet them are the bride-to-be beautifully attired in Chinese *chong sam* and her parents. After some pleasantries, they sit down to a meal of noodle soup. I would suppose that this tradition parallels that of the Filipino tradition called "*pamanhikan*" where the groom and his parents go to the girl's house to ask for her hand in marriage from her parents. The whole affair is extremely formal, colorful, and replete with symbolisms.

I met with the club members who were thrilled with such a novel concept. We spent a number of days preparing for the presentation. I did the anthology and the emceeing portion, and we had an all-girl cast for the show. But during the formal rehearsal, our presentation didn't make much sense because we still didn't have the stage props which were integral to the show. Since there was no dialogue, what the audience saw was just the cast gesticulating and moving around. It didn't make sense at all. My group felt down and depressed. But rather than whine and wallow, we decided to immediately hold a meeting to deal with the situation. What followed was an eye opener for me because I saw how the Chinese students rose to the challenge.

Initially, they decided to scrap the engagement ceremony and start from scratch by presenting a traditional Chinese dance instead. It would be costly, however, because we needed to come up with costumes. But there were members willing to shoulder the cost. As a group we went to St. Stephen's and talked to the teacher who agreed to teach us the dance. Then we went to a nearby dress shop for the costumes. The clothing material was silk with intricate embroideries. It was expensive but a student volunteered to pay for it. The preparatory steps were taken and the girls who would be in the dance were selected. But for some reason, we found out there wouldn't be enough time to learn and rehearse since the program was only around two weeks away. So another meeting was held in which we decided it would be best to go back to the original plan of the engagement ceremony.

This time, we prepared in earnest. Our group was dead serious in doing a good job. A member offered her house where we could do some serious rehearsals. Enthusiastic members volunteered to come up with the props which included traditional ethnic baskets, fruits, sweets and jewelry. The cast even perfected their use of chopsticks because there would be a scene where the engaged couple and their parents would sit down to a meal of noodle soup. For my part I pledged to borrow the living and dining sets from a neighbor who owned a furniture shop in Avenida Rizal. I was delighted when the store owners agreed not only to lend us the sets but allowed us the use of their delivery truck as well. I saw for myself how motivation and organization could move mountains. I was lucky to have such genuinely enthusiastic and resourceful people for my members.

On the night of the gala, our presentation of a Chinese Engagement Ceremony proved to be a huge success. The combination of ingenious characterization where we had girls dressed up in men's costumes to portray the groom and the fathers, the symmetry of the furniture sets, the beautiful *chong sam* costumes of the bride-to-be and the mothers, the big traditional Chinese baskets holding the fruits and other dowries of the groom all managed to bring to life an authentic Chinese tradition. Complete with anthology, the symbolisms of the different elements of the ceremony were explained and opened the eyes of the audience to the richness of this popular tradition. It was something majority of the mostly Filipino audience hadn't seen before. The hearty applause afterwards was truly well deserved.

A year after when I was already in first year college, a Chinese math teacher from high school approached me informing me that the wife of the Chinese ambassador in Manila was looking for me with the request that we present the engagement ceremony once again this time in the name of the Chinese Embassy. The venue would be the Fiesta Pavilion of the Manila Hotel, an illustrious hotel in Manila. This was to be a distinguished event with other embassies coming up with their own national presentations. I was of course taken by surprise although the honor and recognition it brought did not escape me. I was thrilled by the opportunity and agreed to seek out the original members of the cast most of whom were still in high school.

This time around, it was easier for us because the venue for the rehearsals and the costumes and props would all be provided for by the Chinese embassy. We held our rehearsals in the residence of the ambassador and were feted with a sumptuous spread of dimsum and noodles every time. The wife of the ambassador was with us and she helped me recast my piece to further enrich its contents. She talked to me in Mandarin, which I could understand a bit but couldn't really speak fluently. I wrote it in English and when I presented the finished piece to her, she was delighted at its clarity and comprehension, because before then she wasn't quite sure I understood her enough.

The Manila Hotel was truly grand and our group was awed by this singular experience to be able to perform at the Fiesta Pavilion which was its biggest function room.

Needless to say, our presentation went on without a hitch. After the show, a man approached me asking if we could be invited to perform in yet another venue. This time I politely declined.

I ended high school as bronze medalist.

# CCD

"Would you like to join our catechetical group in the parish?" Mang Tony, a neighbor asked Linda and myself while we were outside our house one Sunday afternoon in 1966. "We're looking for catechists and we know you are studying at the UST, so you are both more than qualified to join our team." I was about to enter college that coming school year and Linda was then already working. So we looked at each other and said, "Why not?"

1966 was the beginning of many things in my life. I started college, I started my part time cashiering job at the store, and I joined the catechetical group in our parish, the CCD, short for Confraternity for Christian Doctrine. Sta. Cruz Church was a famous landmark in our area and was just a few blocks away from Avenida Rizal. Run by the Blessed Sacrament Fathers, an American congregation, it was a popular destination for many catholics. And up until then, we were not too aware that we were part of its parochial territory. I remember that we never celebrated the annual fiesta of either Sta. Cruz or Quiapo within which boundaries our house was located. My parents were not active churchgoers then. On the other hand, we children started going to church regularly only when we attended UST where we were initiated into active worship. But aside from Sunday masses, we were not aware of the other activities within the church. Sta. Cruz even then was already a mecca for lay apostolate. We regularly saw ushers in white who would always be around during the mass, but we were just not interested enough to ask about them or to join them.

When Linda and I started volunteer work, we were part of only a handful of catechists who taught for about an hour every Sunday morning at a small school which was actually a school of Optometry within the parish. The children were mostly from the depressed areas of the parish. After Sunday classes, we would troop to the church where the children attended Mass and were given a free meal consisting of milk and biscuits. Basically we prepared them for First Communion which was held around Christmas time every year. Fr. Morin, SSS, was the parish priest at that time and headed the CCD. He was soft spoken and kindly. That Christmas, we saw a lighter side to him when he raffled out gifts to our small group of catechists. I was delighted to have gotten a black crucifix which was a container for holy water as well.

Fr. Donald Jette, SSS, was probably the most popular parish priest we ever had at Sta. Cruz during that time. When he became spiritual director of the CCD, our organization expanded and in time had quite a big population of children from all around the parish attending our Sunday school. The older catechists also trained a number of younger ones, and in time, we became a very active youth organization. Our work also involved going around the mainly impoverished areas of the parish in order to try and bring in more children to our Sunday classes. This gave me a glimpse of how people in marginalized households survive. I was puzzled when a mother once told me the reason why she didn't want her children to join our classes. She said she didn't want her children to keep hearing don'ts and shouldn'ts which she figured were what catechism classes were mainly concerned with. She said it hampered instead of fostering growth. We respected her opinion and didn't counter her arguments. But there were many more parents who were enthusiastic and agreed to send in their children. At the beginning, we had to pick up the children from different neighborhoods and we would proceed to the church in long lines. The children were usually ranked according to age and I discovered I enjoyed handling the younger ones, mostly four and five year olds. Their bright eyes and eagerness to learn and engage was sufficient to make up for the work that we did. I was extremely surprised one time to see a very young girl actually tearing up as I narrated the life and crucifixion of Christ.

Linda and I were part of this group for several years. Espee eventually joined us too and stayed on for many more years even after Linda and I have both left. Our core group became almost inseparable. There were a number of boys and girls of our age who became really close friends, and at least two married each other. Fr. Jette would treat us to lunch most Sundays after our work and our group would continue to hang around singing and playing the guitars in the little office that was given for our use on Sundays. Often to celebrate birthdays, the group would buy chicharon and ice cream and that always made our day. We didn't need to spend much because we enjoyed ourselves a lot. CCD forged a healthy and enthusiastic bond among us teen agers who came from diverse backgrounds, schools, and families. We were at that age when youth, idealism, religion and good clean fun were a premium. Sta. Cruz gave this to us. We were provided a forum where we could feel important and where our voices could be heard, and where we could achieve something worthwhile not only for ourselves but for the less fortunate. It didn't even feel like work. Religion was not just liturgy or dogma. Religion was life itself.

Meanwhile, the different streets around the boundary of the parish were slowly feeling the influence of the church in their daily lives. Fr. Jette has successfully immersed himself in the community, more especially the depressed areas that abounded. He was a dear friend to both the very poor and the very rich. He soon became a regular sight in the streets as he visited the constituents of his parish. His presence as well as the candies in his pocket inevitably drew the children rushing out of their houses to greet him. He spoke Tagalog reasonably well and this endeared him greatly to the Filipinos. One evening, my siblings and I challenged him to eat *balut*, a Filipino delicacy which most foreigners are extremely reluctant to try. We were pretty sure he would not like it and secretly hoped he wouldn't so we could end the episode with a good laugh. To our dismay and amazement, Fr. Jette liked it and asked for more. He ate a total of four *baluts* in one sitting.

Christmas time was fun too because Fr. Jette arranged for the CCD group to carol the homes of his many friends. We had members with fantastic singing voices and a number who played the guitars extremely well. So we had quite a formidable singing group. We got to sing Christmas carols in the houses of rich patrons of the parish who were located in exclusive subdivisions. Being the secretary of the organization, I sent out letters to prospective people whom we intended to carol. We usually managed to fix a schedule which lasted four or five nights. Fr. Jette provided us with transport using a van of the church which he himself drove. We would start at around seven in the evening and would visit three or four houses a night. In every one of these houses, we were served sumptuous snacks. It was truly fun and enjoyable and the CCD bond grew closer with the passing of the years. The proceeds all went to the catechetical funds.

Our group also became almost an extended family and often, when we happened to be at our house, Mama would serve lunch for us. They loved to call my mom "*Nanay*" as well which is Mother in Filipino. Mama did not skimp when it came to feeding our friends. She really enjoyed their company as well. She always had marinated pork in the fridge ready to be fried on occasions like this when unexpected guests like our friends happened to drop by.

Desto, Charito, Odette, Alredo, Elisa, Sison, Ernie, Angge, Ima, Anita, Gilda, Manoling, Susan were just some of our *barkada* (gang). One time Ma said to me "I like to watch americans like Fr. Jette eat. They are so refined and they chew their food with so much finesse." That is when I realized without a shadow of a doubt that Mama gets a lot of satisfaction merely watching people enjoy eating her food. To a cook this is more than enough payment.

Mama and Papa became regular churchgoers during this time. They developed the practice of attending the early morning Sunday mass every week. When we had lauriat celebrations, the Blessed Sacrament Fathers were routinely invited. Once again, food was the tie that was creating the bond and reaching beyond our family.

# College and Beyond

It seems the universe decided to fast track my life when I reached college. I have initially wanted to take up foreign service but a cousin of mine who had taken this course ahead of me advised me not to pursue it because it was difficult to land a job afterwards, as she herself was experiencing. So, looking around, I decided to take up AB Economics, for the simple reason that it was a new course and it sounded like an in thing for the future. So I enrolled at the Faculty of Arts and Letters at the UST, again as a full scholar.

Linda had just graduated from college and was leaving the cashier job at the store. Naturally my father turned to me, the one next in line to render my services. Since my classes were in the morning, I was required to report for work from one o'clock until seven thirty pm, closing time. Thus began my part time job as a cashier.

It was enjoyable, too, because life was never dull in the midst of downtown Avenida. I got to experience the sights and sounds of a throbbing city life. People of all shapes and sizes, rich and poor, young and old, in a never ending stream pass this way. The street vendors who litter the sidewalks showed me a side of life where resiliency is key. The constant hide and seek with the policeman is a game that they seem to enjoy playing. Often enough, a sleepy afternoon would be shattered by the loud shriek of the policeman's whistle, a sound that would send the vendors scampering for cover because they're simply not allowed to set up shop on the sidewalks but they do anyway. Some get caught. Many others manage to escape with a number of tricks up their sleeves. Their wares which moments before are spread for all to see would in a snap turn into a wooden briefcase safely tucked up under their arms as they pretend to walk along with other passersby.

Around this period, the Nora Aunor phenomenon was taking shape. Nora Aunor was a poor girl from Bicol province who was thrust into the Philippine cinema scene where she grew bigger than life. Her fine singing voice and her background of rural poverty was something that the masses easily identified with and pretty soon, she had turned into a blockbuster star. It so happened that her promoter, a radio personality named Inday Badiday held shop at a radio station located at the Republic Supermarket which was right along Soler where our store was situated. Every single afternoon right around noontime, hundreds of fans would start gathering at this tiny street leading up to the radio station. The reason was because Nora Aunor would be at the Inday Badiday radio program. The fans would gather there every day, and Sun Hee, who was a really quiet person, was extremely puzzled. What was the fuss all about? Of course he was not vocal about his curiosity, but one day he just blurted out "So, that is what is the matter! It is that tiny girl! That is whom they are all so crazy about!" He finally figured it all out. The superstar "Nora Aunor" eventually became not only a singing sensation but went on to become one of the country's finest actresses with a number of national and international trophies to her name.

It was easy to be a working student in college during the sixties mainly because classes were in block sections meaning one is either a morning student, an afternoon student, or an evening student. Not much time was wasted in idle hours at school. And it freed me for entire mornings or afternoons which gave me room to work part time. It also gave me ample time to devote to catechetical work in the parish on Sundays. Extra-curricular work enabled me to hone my writing skills as well. My theology professor assigned me to do some feature writing in the newsletter of the Santissimo Rosario Church within UST. At that time I was also doing feature writing for the Adorer newsletter of Sta. Cruz parish. I enjoyed these forays into writing which involved interviewing different personalities of various nationalities. I was privileged to do write ups on the museum director of UST, as well as a number of American officials of the Blessed Sacrament Fathers who occasionally visited the Philippines, priests of the congregation and their religious friends, as well as lay leaders of the different parish organizations. "People find it easy to open up to you" Fr. George, my spiritual director, remarked as my articles regularly appeared.

College life was fun, too. First two years were generally just a summation of basic math, English and science subjects taken up during high school, plus the required Spanish and theology units. Third and fourth year zeroed in on philosophy and subjects related to one's major field of study. I didn't regret taking up Economics and enjoyed particularly the macroeconomics subjects. I especially liked the deductive and inductive reasoning that came with the discipline of the course. For me it was the social aspects of economics that held more allure. Since economics is not an exact science, it was fun to tackle the essay parts of exams and termpapers although one needed to be astute as well on the mathematical and statistical parts of it in order to understand its social implications.

Terry, my seatmate during my third and fourth year remained a close friend even after graduation. Seating was alphabetical and we were seatmates during the last two years of college. Terry normally brings a sandwich with her everyday. Because they owned a grocery store, her sandwich always boasted of a thick pile of cold cuts. She would always share a half of her sandwich with me. Although I was friends with the rest of the class, Terry and I belonged to a close knit group of six Chinese girls who liked to hang out together. We were a conscientious, studious bunch and needless to say clannish as the Chinese normally are. When one of our group brings *dikiam* (Chinese sweet preserves), she wanted it to be shared only among us. The rest of the class was automatically excluded. And when one of us has her birthday, our group liked to celebrate at Savory chicken restaurant in Escolta. Terry and I used to go home together. We would ride the same *jeepney* at Dapitan. I get off earlier than her. It became an unspoken practice between us that we would take turns paying the fare. One time when the class went on an excursion, Terry and I bought fresh coconuts to bring home. We realized our mistake when we alighted from the chartered bus to take another jeepney for home. By then we were dead tired and found that lugging our backpacks and three heavy coconuts each was no joke. Such a lesson one never forgets.

I finished my AB Economics course and graduated Summa Cum Laude, an event which meant a lauriat celebration once again. Papa was with me when I received the Rector's Academic Excellence Award and again during the graduation ceremony, when I received the coveted Gold Medal. Mama was with us as well as Fr. Jette. It was an honor for me to deliver the Baccalaureate Speech, and as an add-on Papa gave a celebratory party for my classmates in the beautiful house of my *Di-E* (Second Aunt). When I saw that the feast included giant prawns, I knew how much pride and honor I have given Mama and Papa. This time I have really done them proud and I was real happy.

# Christmas at the Ong's

Deck the halls with boughs of holly…fa la la la la lalalala….Tis the season to be jolly…fa la la la la lalalala…goes the joyous Christmas carols. It is the evening of December 24 and at the stroke of midnight we are still awake and partaking of our Noche Buena, a Filipino tradition of Christmas eve meal. We have Chinese ham, *queso de bola*, bread, butter, hot chocolate, fruits, and sweet desserts. Papa brings home a whole leg of Chinese ham every Christmas season. This is usually purchased cured and wrapped in wax paper but not yet cooked. For a fee, Pa would have it cooked at the luncheonette across our store in Avenida. What comes out is a golden ham with sugary sweet burnt surface revealing underneath it a soft delectable fat layer cradling a pinkish salty bed of lean meat. Placed on a festive rectangular platter, this luscious ham crowns the Christmas table of most Filipino homes. Holding the bone with one hand, Ma would carve this into extra thin slices and layer it accordion style. We loved to make sandwiches out of it with sprinklings of sugar to make it more yummy. For Papa, Ma would go further and pan fry the ham slices in a little cooking oil to bring out the crispness of the ham before she fills the bread with it. Chinese ham is delicious. And we only got to eat it during Christmas.

As with many Christmases, our three spinster grannies (unmarried sisters of my grandmother on my mother's side) Lola Binday, Lola Mary, and Lola Alying are all spending the night in our house. Mama invites them every year to help prepare the big spread of fiesta foods in our house for Christmas day. Lola Binday is bespectacled, short and smiles a lot. Lola Mary is also short, with a small face holding her spectacles while Lola Alying is a no nonsense person housing a cheerful personality beneath. All three of them have remained unmarried and lived together. They spent most of their adult lives working in an umbrella factory. Mama solicits their help during Christmas to make the meticulous dessert dishes like leche flan, macapuno, and sweet beans. They're also tasked with preparing the beef morcon. This dish requires a lot of patience to prepare. It is actually thinly sliced beef round which is rolled and stuffed with pickles, olives, hard boiled eggs, and red bell pepper, and tied up with a thin cloth string. It is then stewed for about an hour and then cooled. Sliced into rounds with the stuffings peeking out in a window, it is a beautiful dish with Christmas colors of green, yellow, and red.

Rising real early on Christmas morning, Mama would complete her repertoire of dishes by finishing her other dishes. We always had *lechon*, fried chicken, *pancit sotanghon*, *hi chi* (a chicken stew with sharks' fins), meat balls, and soup. Mama was always careful to cook enough because being a cook, *long phua tianh* is a disaster she never wanted to suffer. This means not having enough food for the invited guests.

Every Christmas, it has been a tradition in the family to hold a day-long celebration at home. As children, we did not experience the practice of going to other people's houses for Christmas like many other children. In the Philippines, it was customary for children to go to their godparents' home for gifts and eats. But since Mama always has the party at home, other people come to the house instead to celebrate. Mama's many godchildren including those of her *sukis* in the market would come at different hours of the day but mostly during lunch. Mama has her gifts all wrapped up for her godchildren. Papa's friends also come around and we're always excited for this because we are sure to be handed our gifts in the form of money. Some of our aunts and uncles also come around and sometimes, an aunt's suitor would give us money to watch movies in the afternoon.

As soon as they notice that Papa is already up, a number of men line up outside our door asking for their Christmas gifts. These are mostly our neighbor's drivers and vendors in Avenida, as well as the down-and-outs in the neighborhood who have become part of the familiar tableau in Mabolo. Papa would good-naturedly hand them a few bucks each hoping they would use this to buy themselves some additional food. However, we were usually not surprised to see them minutes later lighting firecrackers and drinking beer instead.

I remember that the first visitors to usually arrive on Christmas day were Papa's Chinese godson and his wife. They would come at around ten o'clock in the morning bringing their gifts for Papa. We learned from Mama that although it is customary for our godparents to give gifts to us during Christmas, we have to remember that this practice is reversed when we become adults. Then it would be our turn to give gifts to our godparents. This is the Chinese way, she says.

Mama's preparation for her gift giving happens a few weeks before Christmas. I remember that the two of us would hie off to Central Market for the needed shopping. Before the advent of shopping malls, Central Market was the place to go to when one needs to buy ready-made dresses for children. It is similar to the *tiangges* (flea markets) of today where there are individual stalls carrying various merchandise ranging from bags, slippers, shoes, dusters, dresses, pants, fans, accessories, cosmetics, beauty products, etc. Mama and I usually leave the house around three o'clock in the afternoon and oftentimes the two of us just walk the distance to go there. We usually go directly to the stalls where there are a lot of pretty embroidered and laced girl's dresses. I loved to observe Mama expertly haggling her way and often we manage to clinch delightfully low priced dresses and clothes for her many "*inaanak*" or godchildren. I learned from these situations that it is almost a must to bargain as the encounter gives both buyer and seller an emotional high. I also learned that oftentimes a buyer would feel almost cheated if the seller gives in right away to her request for a stated lower price. She ends up feeling she should have bid for a lower price. This conflicted sense of having won and lost at the same time is unique to the Filipino practice of haggling in the marketplace. I enjoy these shopping expeditions with Mama and they always succeed in putting me in a holiday spirit just in time for Christmas. Clutching the many paper bags of newly bought clothes which oftentimes includes a piece for myself, Mama and I walk home tired but satisfied.

A few days before Christmas, Papa would buy large cartons of apples, pears, and grapes. Then on the 24th of December, he would open these boxes and start putting together several baskets containing an assortment of these fruits. He sometimes also adds in a giftwrapped leg of uncooked ham. These are gifts to our family doctor and his and mama's wedding godparents. For these trips, he would bring one or two of my brothers along. When they come home, my brothers would proudly show us the "*angpao*" or Christmas money that they received in turn.

On Christmas day, a number of my Papa's good friends come by and we were sure to be handed cash if we happened to be up and around at that time. When I started working at the family store, I was usually bone tired by Christmas day because of the extra hours of work for the month preceding that I often spent the entire morning sleeping and would wake up only in the afternoon when most of the guests have already eaten and left. By this time, only Mama would be eating because she liked to take her time eating and that is when almost all the guests have left. I would take my seat beside her and start my own feast. At this time we would already have the spin off dish from *lechon* (pig roast) which is what I enjoy most and that is *lechon paksiw*. The *lechon* is chopped into bite size pieces including the bones and the skin. Garlic and onions are first sauted after which the *lechon* is put inside a casserole. Added to this is a handful of oregano leaves and whole peppercons, white vinegar, salt, sugar, the *lechon* sauce, and water. Often Mama would add in a whole bottle of Mang Tomas *lechon* sauce for a more substantial sauce. Together with *patis* and white rice, this always made my day.

I remember one Christmas when I got my hand burned because of playing with firecrackers. These came in the form of small pinhead rounds on a red sheet of paper. There would be as many as twenty rounds in one sheet. We use a small pebble to pound on these pins to make them explode. I remember carrying one of these sheets in my hand and as I passed by the door, the whole sheet exploded. My hand got burned. This traumatized me for life and I never lighted another firecracker ever again.

Christmas always brought a lot of family and friends to our house. Oftentimes during these events, Papa would bring out the long wooden sofa to the sidewalk outside our door. There are so many visitors we needed more room to move around in the house. So the guests literally spill out onto the streets. It's the same thing with our neighbors. Every house has a party going on as well. It is good to see our friends and playmates all dressed in holiday attire and having fun.


Whereas Christmas was always celebrated at home, New Year is something that calls for a *lauriat* celebration. Pa is normally frugal but he believes that *lauriat* celebration is a necessary expenditure for the family and brings in good fortune with it. He is fond of saying *tsieng kieng khai tio khai* meaning there are certain necessary things in life one needs to spend for. Papa reserves two or three tables for the occasion. As the grandchildren came one after the other, the number of tables increased. We all looked forward to these celebrations. Oftentimes there was no need to invite guests aside from the family because the family has grown exponentially because of the grandchildren. Usually we would all be coming from our parent's home where we have all gathered first. Arriving at the restaurant almost at the same time, everyone gets into a celebratory mood. There is a lot of ribbing and camaraderie as we settle down to the hearty feast ahead. The children never really eat much in the lauriat. They are more excited to get off their chairs at the first opportunity and run around. No worries though, because Mama knew just how to tackle the leftovers. She would store them in the fridge and the next day, she would mix them all up in a giant casserole. Chicken, seafoods, veggies, sticky rice, sauces from different dishes are all poured into one pot and are heated up, and we come up with "*tsapchai*" meaning ten dishes. I think Ma really means *chopsuey* which is simply a dish which calls for different kinds of viands mixed together in a colorful and delicious hash. Thus, another joyous occasion comes to pass.

The happy colors of Christmas and New Year, music, family, friends, laughter, good food, gifts, and fun….. these are the images of the yuletide season that I grew up with. Life was full of meaning. There was community and feasting. Rejoicing was part of life.

# Farewell, Mama and Papa

One by one, we the sons and daughters of Mariano and Sion left our family home to get married and formed our own families. All of us finished college and held degrees in Medicine, Engineering, Nursing, Economics, Commerce, Banking and Finance, Business Administration, and Entrepreneurship. Several of us graduated from college with honors. Bongga finished his Chemical Engineering degree with a Cum Laude honor. Espee graduated Cum Laude from Nursing. Danny and Linda missed it by a few points. We all did well in our studies and went on to find jobs in our respective careers. Our parents gave us a free hand in choosing our careers and life partners and for several of us, the process was not easy for them because it defied tradition and at times commonly accepted norms. But through it all, they showed unconditional support in our choices and the options we took. They have time and again proven true to their own adage *tsi lang um tsai ianh tsi lang eh tai*. Many times they could not fully understand but trusted that the children they raised were responsible adults. And indeed, we did not disappoint them. All became responsible parents, and all, no matter what the circumstances in their own lives, carried on the tradition of seeing to it that all of their own children went on to finish college.

As the grandchildren arrived, Aling Sion found her house filled not only with her nine children but their children as well, and Sundays became days of constant reunions and celebrations. She laughingly remarked that her cooking job has grown harder through the years because her brood has expanded so much. But she continued to delight herself with feeding her many grandchildren who have taken to her cooking so much they all looked forward to Sundays when they could get a taste of their "*lola's*" *adobo, bolabola, pancit*, etc. which have become their favorites as well. Mama, at times, had to hide some of her apos' favorite dishes like the crisp, golden fried meatballs so that the children won't finish them off before lunch. But my two small daughters knew just where the favorite hiding place of this dish is and *Lola* would amusedly let them have a few pieces.

Sundays were also mahjong days for the family with Papa and Mama playing with my brothers and sisters and our in-laws to while away the lazy hours of Sundays. I once overheard Pa and Ma talking with each other and musing that when the two of them get to be too old and weak to work, would their children come to the fore and take care of them? Or would they, like a number of others, beg off hoping that since there are so many of them, the others would hopefully take up the cudgel? This is a common worry among many seniors. But Ma passed away before this necessity could arise. She died of a heart attack at the age of seventy-five.

Both Mama and Papa were blessed with a peaceful death. Both of them were surrounded by family when their final moments came. Mama had been hospitalized several times and in all this time, her cardiologist has always jokingly advised her to take a rest from all the cooking she has been doing. I was with her in one of her extended hospital stays and the intern who was wheeling her to the laboratory remarked to me that he has never met such a cheerful, pleasant patient. Even in her room, Mama was generous with the plentiful food and snacks her children brought and would often share them with her nurses. Papa was also getting sickly and had just come home from a hospital stay when Ma suffered her final cardiac arrest. Danny, perhaps knowing this could be the end, asked the hospital staff to just confine her at a private room instead of wheeling her to the ICU, where her children would not be allowed in. He then asked that the necessary cardiac resuscitation machines be brought to the room. We were at her bedside in no time at all and kept watch during the night. Linda noticed that during this trip to the hospital, she didn't feel the inclination to arrange Mama's personal items which they brought from home as she has always done before. Mama was conscious but could not talk with a tube placed inside her throat. That evening, she suffered her final cardiac arrest and we stood around her as we waited for her ECG to register a straight line. When I told Papa the sad news, Papa fell on his knees and sobbed. This was the first time I saw him totally devastated and crying in anguish. But ever the deeply disciplined man he has been all his life, he rose to the occasion and saw to the arrangements which was the last service he needed to offer his wife.

The funeral rites lasted one week and it was a glorious celebration instead of a mourning event. Mass was held each evening with the Blessed Sacrament fathers offering the Mass. With so many children and grandchildren, every day at Arlington Memorial was like a fiesta celebration. Many came to condole with the family. Papa had to get the largest viewing room at Arlington to accommodate all the people who came each day to share this moment of passing.

The line of children, grandchildren and friends who walked the path at the cemetery was long. But rather than a sorrowful procession, it was an uplifting sight to behold so many in white accompanying my Mom to her final resting place. And at the gate of the Chinese Cemetery in Manila, all of us, Papa, children, and grandchildren knelt at the entrance to pay our last tribute to a great wife, mother and grandmother.

Papa died five years after at the age of seventy-seven. They were so close, Papa knew he would soon follow Mama. He asked the lord to give him five more years to bring his life to a proper closure. At this time, fate decided to usher in another blessing to the Ong family. People say that when God closes a door, He opens another window.

So true. At this time, Eddie has separated from his first wife. His second wife Tess and their children came to live with Papa. Tess proved to be a wonderful daughter-in-law. When Papa got seriously sick, he was blest with the personal care not only of Danny, but also of Tess who served as his faithful nurse throughout. She also loved to cook and this endeared her to Papa. Needless to say, the presence of Danny made it a lot easier for Pa in his final days.

Papa was finally diagnosed with COPD due to emphysema. Whenever he was confined, the steady stream of children and grandchildren made it seem more like a party than anything else. Everyone who comes to visit at all hours of the day would bring some food. I guess this greatly lightened the load on Papa in spite of the severity of his illness. Enyong and Eddie would take turns staying with him for the night. And when finally, the doctor announced he could no longer do anything short of a lung transplant, Papa went back home. This time, Danny took over his care. He had two large oxygen tanks installed in Pa's room and a male worker at the store was hired to help care for him 24/7. Papa became totally bedridden and had periodic flare ups which required an IV through which Danny placed needed antibiotics. This would time and again miraculously cure him. Linda cheered him up by playing cards of solitaire for him. I remember with amusement that one time, when I was there and opted to play the solitaire card game, he quickly shooed me off when Linda arrived because he said I was too slow. "Linda does it better." Sundays were once again noisy days when all the grandchildren would come and Papa would be totally surrounded as the whole gang stayed in his room to watch the noontime variety shows on television. Evenings saw Eddie and his three young children keeping Papa company by watching television in his room before he goes to sleep.

I once remarked to Danny that he was creating another specialty carreer as he managed to keep Papa alive with his magic touch. But he said he much prefers pediatrics to geriatrics. It was undoubtedly the constant and faithful presence of his favorite doctor son that kept Papa's spirit up. And Danny managed to keep him alive for six more months. It was a hopeful period for the family as we clung on to the hope that by some miracle, Papa would go back to full health. However, it was at the same time heart wrenching to see him hooked full time to the oxygen tank and in spite of this to watch him belaboring to breathe. His throat seems to register this incessant painful activity and I used to liken this to a cylinder that is endlessly straining to move up and down, up and down, afraid that at any moment it could just give up and explode. Pa has lost so much weight he looked more like a shadow of his former self.

I made it a point to spend whole Sundays with him and certain weekdays as well. He seemed always happy to see me. Once I came while he and Linda and Tess's mother were playing mahjong. I was surprised to note that he immediately packed up the game to welcome me. He told me he was already like a child now eager to just talk and connect. He probably found it calming that I was comfortable talking about death and dying. I shared with him things I have read about the subject especially the works of Raymond Moody and Elizabeth Kubler Ross who have both written extensively about near death experiences. I assured him that I had no doubt life beyond death would be extremely good way beyond our wildest imagination. I even said that when he reaches heaven, I would be grateful if he visits me and tell me how it is. When Fr. Ginthoer, a good friend, came to administer the Sacrament of the Sick on Papa, he confided to the priest that he was ready to die, but inspite of this he didn't know why he still felt so much fear. To which Fr. Ginthoer said that when the final moment comes, it is the Lord Himself who will come to him and bring him home. Papa received Holy Communion and I believe was greatly comforted.

On the last flare up of his disease, Papa refused to allow Danny to administer the regular IV antibiotic treatment. He has seen the pattern of his disease, and no longer desired to be kept alive longer. I was with him on his last day. Danny seemed uncharacteristically uneasy and moody. Being a doctor, he knew deep inside himself that the end is very near. Papa's voice that day sounded oddly guttural and broken. It was only later that I learned from Danny that this was the death rattle commonly seen in dying patients. When I left to go home, Tess brought Papa his dinner. She recounted that as she was about to feed him, Papa shifted his glance to the door of his room, stared at it for a moment, and was gone. Since it was already evening and Arlington Memorial has said it would be better to just fetch Papa's remains in the morning, all of us children and grandchildren, stayed at Papa's room to begin the long novena prayers for the dead. As in life, so in death, family kept him company.

With the opening of Manila to the light rail transit system, overhead rails were built along Avenida Rizal which darkened the horizon in the once bright and cheerful ambiance of the bustling downtown. Business took a sharp downturn and our textile store had to close off the long front part leaving only a small space at the end. Even this was not enough to save the business and the store had to shut down completely when Papa died.

"Life is a journey." Was Danny's simple answer to *Di-E* (our aunt) when the latter asked him what life is all about. As a doctor, Danny has witnessed life's most poignant moments from the birth of a baby to the death of the sick and the elderly. This must have equipped him with an inner knowing that life is a process which does not end with dying. At the same time it must have given him a priceless peak into the ever constant awe and wonderment in the eyes of a child. And his brief statement, I believe, sums up the core lesson his profession has gifted him with. This is perhaps the reason why he did not fight the first and final cardiac arrest that hit him, but instead succumbed peacefully into it. He died young at the age of fifty-three. Carol, the youngest daughter and the prettiest of the brood, succumbed to cancer also at the young age of fifty-four. Another brother, Bobby, died abroad at an equally young age of forty-two.

Mariano and Sion continue to live on in our memories and in our everyday lives as we try to raise our own families in the same tradition of love, nourishment, and good name above all. And food continues to be the gel that binds our respective lives. Nothing really dies, because the memories live on and continue to find expression in the generations that follow.

# And the Celebration Continues

I just opened facebook and saw Eddie's post of the food offerings for Papa's death anniversary. Papa and Mama loved to say when they were still living that "s*i lang kue ke did*" meaning "the dead passes time quickly". Mama has been dead 24 years and Papa 19 years. But Eddie and his family where the pictures of Ma and Pa are prominently placed in a revered place in the family's dining room celebrate these anniversaries without fail, including their birthdays, Christmas, New Year, and All Saints' Day. Alongside these pictures are also the pictures of my brothers Danny and Bobby and sister Carol who have since also passed away. These pictures of our dead have been there ever since they each passed away. It is our belief that as much as possible, they should not be moved. Eddie sometimes offers sampaguita flowers for them. And a votive lamp is kept burning day and night. Special mass for the dead is offered during their birth and death anniversaries as well.

Espee, a nurse based in the states, always makes sure that she sends additional money to Eddie to do the *"alay"* as we call it during these times of the year, and again during All Saints' Day. Several dishes are served on the table with plates and silverware corresponding to the number of the departed close family members. The incense holder is taken down and placed on the table as well. Then the family makes the usual incense lighting and bowing before the pictures of the deceased after which the incense sticks are placed in the holder and allowed to burn until they are extinguished. The family cannot begin eating until after the deceased have finished their meal. To know when this happens, Eddie would toss two coins. If the coins end up with either both tail or both head, this means the deceased have finished eating. Otherwise, we have to wait until the tossing of the coins renders the desired result. Sometimes this takes quite a while, and we would laughingly conclude that the dead are still enjoying their food and company.

Mariano and Sion started out as a married couple. They successfully raised nine children all of whom fulfilled their dream – that of graduating from college and responsibly raising their own families. Their journey is a testament to the strength of conviction and purpose of the human spirit. Grounded on a good name above all, a good life is a priceless legacy to the generations that follow.

In this manner, our parents continue to permeate our lives. As I have said before, our family does not adhere strictly to traditions of religion and culture. But there are certain rituals that we deem necessary to continue. The revering of ancestors was a singular practice that Papa has observed all his life. He was of the firm belief that the proper burial and commemoration of one's parents is necessary to smoothen the lives of succeeding generations as well as to continue the blessings for the entire family. In this area, we have deemed it proper to continue the tradition of remembering, honoring, and celebrating the dead. Food has been at the cornerstone of all our celebrations as a family. It is both a celebration and a blessing.

*Lydia Calasanz*

Remembering Mama, Bobby, Papa, Danny, and Carol

And food says it all (lovingly prepared by Eddie and Tess)

# About the Author

Lydia Calasanz discovers that revisiting one's past offers a privileged view unlike any other. One is at a vantage point where the seemingly mundane happenings in life literally explode to expose the hidden gifts they have been carrying all along. Being part of a big family carries its own advantage of discovering the sameness in diversity – the driving force and purpose that defines character – and the eyes with which to see these precious gems. This is her first book. Lydia has two daughters and lives with her husband in the State of Washington.